Legacy

THE LOST ART OF

Blessing

BY: DEBBIE KITTERMAN

Scriptures with bolded portions are to express emphasis by the author.
Please take note that the name of satan and related names are not capitalized. The author chooses not to give him importance.

Cover design and book layout by Brandi Kitterman, Create Media

Dedication

To my children, future grandchildren, and beyond. You are my legacy to the world. This book and all I have taught and imparted to you over the years is my legacy to you. God has called our family to be a family who leaves a legacy for others. Our legacy is not just for our family, but for all the families we connect with and the communities in which we live.

Remember, YOU ARE A GIFT which God has given to the world! It is my prayer you walk with Jesus and fulfill all His plans for your lives and our family's lives. I bless you to live a long, fruitful, and faith-filled life. You are a *gift* to the world and those whom you meet. May God's hand of favor rest upon you and be evident to all who interact with you. May He richly bless every area of your life and may you be a blessing to others.

To those who have passed their legacy on to me: Papa Carl, Pastor Jerry Tyler, and Dad (Thomas McEldowney). You may be gone from this earth but I know you are cheering me on from the cloud of witnesses. I love and miss you all like crazy. I am forever grateful for the Spiritual Legacy you imparted to me. I am doing my best to steward it well and pass it on to future generations.

Contents

Acknowledgments

Holy Spirit: You are my best friend. I can't imagine living life without You. Holy Spirit, you make everything fun and exciting, even if at first, it's terrifying. This book couldn't come to fruition without You. Partnering with You to author this book has been an honor and a privilege. Thank you for helping me steward this God-given message over the years.

John: I love you deeply. You are amazing. Thank you for always championing me and supporting me. You are one of the most patient men I know, besides my dad, which is a good match for me. I am sorry for the times when I may have frustrated you to no end with my wild faith and big dreams, but you always looked for a way (and still do) to help me reach them. We've lived a lot of life together and I couldn't imagine journeying through this life without you by my side. I'm looking forward to this next season together and seeing what God wants to accomplish through our obedience and faith. With what God has shown me, the legacy we leave for our family will be unfathomable.

Mom: You are an inspiration. You challenge me and others around you to go deeper in our faith and spend more time with the Lord. I love your heart for intercession and ministry to others. I am amazed at your bravery to join us and move across the country after living so many years in one location. Since we lost daddy, I know things haven't always been easy, but you have faced them and accomplished a lot. I want you to know this; you are braver than you know, and your courage and bravery inspire others. I love you!

Donna & Carl Sagerser: Donna, I love you more than words could ever express. The years of friendship with you and Papa Carl have made me who I am today. Your love, support, and wisdom have helped me through some of the most difficult and exciting parts of my journey with God. Papa Carl, I miss you every single day. I cherish the long hours of conversation and all the times you challenged me to be better and do better. This teaching on blessings has developed over the years, but you were an integral part of its inception.

Amy Viser: You are a Godsend! You deserve an extra special shoutout. If I could, I would stand on the rooftop and shout about how amazing you are! Thank you for the endless hours of helping to finetune this manuscript. Your thoughts and insight were most helpful. Thank you for all you have done to help me get this baby across the finish line. I am blessed beyond belief by your friendship and your generosity. I love who God has created you to be. You have a huge heart and deep passion for Jesus. Thank you for all your love and support.

Special thanks to Pastor Gary Fishman for sharing your knowledge of Jewish tradition and culture with me.

Pastor Fred and Melynda Rabinovitz, I am forever grateful for your friendship and the opportunities you gave me. Pastor Fred thank you for also sharing your knowledge of Jewish tradition and culture with me.

Special thanks to all those who read early versions of this manuscript, but especially Robynne Miller, Amy Viser, Jennifer and Jeff Wedan, Lauren Guimmarra, and Amie Rogers. Thank you for your dedication, love, and help in fine-tuning my manuscript.

The Remnant Community: Thank you for being my tribe. I love how God has grown our community as we go deeper in the prophetic and build profound relationships. I just want to say a special thank you for all your prayers and encouragement as I was writing and editing this book. They made an enormous difference and I felt them. Thank you!

Thank you to all my Dare 2 Hear ministry supporters, my faithful friends, followers, readers, class participants, and podcast listeners! Your stories, comments, questions, and testimonies have encouraged and inspired me. Much love to you all!

Introduction

The book you hold in your hands has been more than seventeen years in the making.

How can that be, you ask? Simply put–LIFE.

The deeper explanation is a little more complicated and delay is what happens when fear, doubt, unbelief, insecurities, and lies of the enemy run rampant. It happens when all these things are given space to grow louder than what God is saying, hindering us from walking in obedience to God's call.

In 2010 one of my spiritual grandmothers knew I planned to write a book on speaking and pronouncing blessings. She liked my teaching and invited me to participate in a Bible Study connected to Kerry Kirkwood's new book, *The Power of the Blessing*. She felt the book might be insightful and good "research."

As I began reading the book, I remember thinking I had delayed obeying God so long He probably gave the message of "blessing" to someone else. Even though I learned a lot from reading Kerry's book and while we approached the subject from entirely different angles, I immediately threw in the towel, putting the idea on the shelf. That was it—end of story. No one needed me to author a book on blessings. I felt I had missed my window of opportunity from God, and He moved on to someone willing, obedient, and much more qualified than I was.

Have you ever felt that way?

Writing has been something I have longed to do since I was a child. When asked what I wanted to be when I grew up, my answer was always the same: I wanted to be a wife, mother, and writer. As a young child, and into my high school days, I wrote poetry and creative stories. I loved history and romance. I longed to write historical romance novels with a Christian bent. But I was told there was no such thing as a Christian romance novel. This was long before Francine Rivers came on the scene and "those" types of books didn't exist back then. My mother was horrified by the idea. She pictured Harlequin novels exuding steamy sex scenes immersed in Christian-speak. What would her friends think? What would our family think? What would God think?

I gave up on writing historical romance almost as soon as I entered college. While I took history and an elective writing course my first year, it was the writing class that would change the trajectory of my life and become an area the enemy constantly used to remind me of my inadequacies, whispering lies I was all too quick to believe.

Before entering college, I wrote poetry and short stories. I even won some awards for them. I always dreaded the red pen correction marks. Punctuation, grammar, and verb tenses were never my strength, but I was a great storyteller.

However, one particular day during my college writing class everything changed. I remember this day so vividly. The class had gathered into small critique groups and the professor was handing back our papers. As she passed my paper to me, she commented for all to hear, "I'm not sure what you are thinking, but you cannot write. You have no business taking this writing class." She continued on but these statements were all I heard, and they were death to me. I held back tears and as soon as class was over, I fled to the admissions office and immediately dropped the class. I made a vow to NEVER write creatively again. Not even in a journal.

Why I waited for class to end before leaving is beyond me. Shock, horror, shame, and embarrassment rooted me in my seat. I didn't want to draw more attention to myself but at the same time, I refused to give my instructor the satisfaction of leaving in the middle of the session. The damage was done.

It took years of healing and deliverance ministry to overcome that one moment of my life. Yet, it became much more than one moment. Those words caused tremendous damage and opened a spiritual door for the enemy, the father of lies, to continue causing torment and disappointment in my life. I bought into those public comments, believing I was truly unqualified. It was the ruin of my little girl dreams and desires. But God...

It took over fifteen years before I received enough healing and realized I had believed a lie. I chose to believe God instead. It took a sheer act of obedience to pick up my pen and write for the very first time after that college encounter. Silencing the lies and standing on God's truth was a constant battle. I recited and spoke truth from Scripture and reminded myself constantly of the words He spoke to my heart. I wrote promises and declarations on my mirror with a dry-erase pen affirming my call and ability to remind myself multiple times a day.

I never in a million years would have thought I'd end up writing non-fiction. In the early 2000s, when I first developed my teaching on *Speaking and Pronouncing Blessings*, it was not my intent to write a companion book or any other book for that matter. But I did. I self-published a prophetic training manual, wrote my first book which was also self-published, and later picked up by Chosen Books as an updated version. Truth be told, God told me to author the book you are reading now long before I ever wrote my manual or the other books which followed. And so, this book is a labor of love, springing from the devastation caused by thoughtless words so long ago.

The enemy knows the power of words and especially how effective they can be when spoken, pronounced, and declared. But words coming from our heavenly Father spring from His very heart and mind giving them exponential power. They leave a lasting legacy for those who receive them, grab hold of them, and steward them to their fruition.

In Scripture, the very first blessing we read about was pronounced over the creatures of the sea and birds of the air.

> *And God blessed them, saying, "Be fruitful and multiply and fill the waters in the seas, and let the birds multiply on the earth."*
> Gen 1:22 ESV

And God carries this practice out through the Bible. Yet somewhere along the way, we lost sight and understanding of the importance of what a blessing is. They are not just mere words spoken we "hope" God will do something with. No, they are powerful, can be prophetic in nature, serve to impart hope, and give life to those who receive them. Blessings are important to God. When we bless others as Scripture intends, we release the power of God into their lives. When given to others, they are not just for the individual but for an entire family line for generations to come. We see the legacy of the Scriptural blessings God spoke over Adam and Eve to "be fruitful and multiply" still in effect today. The very act of speaking and pronouncing blessings to others has become somewhat of a lost art today. But we can regain what was lost and begin to walk in the fullness of this powerful gift from God.

Often in our world today, when we think of blessing, we define it as prosperity or wealth, but a blessing is so much more. Just like the words **inheritance** and **legacy**, we are conditioned to think of them only in the monetary sense. If we only think of them as one-dimensional, we are missing out on a crucial element of their far-reaching potential and power.

As you read this book, I pray you will understand the importance of blessing and also feel encouraged and equipped to begin to bless others. We can bless our family, our pastors, our friends, government leaders, people in authority, and anyone else for whom we pray. But let's not stop there. Jesus was intentional in sharing and spreading the good news of the gospel in the marketplace and we should be too. He went beyond just speaking kind and affirming words to others and we can too. Like Jesus, let's begin to bless those we connect with in the world today.

As you read this book, think of blessings as having multiple layers. Blessings need to be accessible to everyone, so start where you are. At the basic level, blessings begin with speaking kind, encouraging, and affirming words. The next level is intentionally speaking or pronouncing a blessing by using Scripture or a Biblical concept as your starting point. This is followed then by the prophetic blessings.

In later chapters, I will discuss more in-depth the prophetic nature of blessings and how they can impact others. As you step out in blessing others, you will see a blending of all three, and sometimes it's hard to see where the delineations are. Much like a swimming pool with a shallow, middle, and deep end, there is a gradual incline from one to the other. It's hard to distinguish where one stops and the other starts. The same is true with affirming words, blessings, and prophetic blessings.

Here are some samples taken from Psalm 90:17:

> *Let the favor of the Lord our God be upon us, and establish the work of our hands upon us; yes, establish the work of our hands. (ESV)*

- Kind and affirming words
  - ° I can see the hand and favor of the Lord resting upon your life.
- Intentional Blessing:
  - ° May you continue to increase in the Lord's favor and may others to see and know His hand is resting upon your life
- Prophetic Blessing:
  - ° Everything you put your mind and hand to will succeed because the Lord's favor is upon you and His hand rests on you.

Reading and pronouncing the blessings of the Bible are no longer daily habits or occurrences. Of more concern is our lack of hearing from God about what we should speak and how we can use our prophetic voice to release blessings over others.

As in my previous books, you will find exercises designed to help you initiate the Art of Blessing others. At the end of each chapter, you'll discover sections I call "Legacy Builders," which contain questions, prayers, and activations. I want these sections to serve as tools to activate you. An activation is a simple exercise aiding you in implementing and practicing the art of blessing. I not only want to teach but also motivate you to engage in the very thing you read.

Chapter 1
Our Words Open Spiritual Doors

Death and Life are in the power of the tongue…
Proverbs 18:21 NKJV

Scripture confirms how powerful our words are. But how often do we intentionally utilize or place our words so that they open spiritual doors in the lives of others?

There is power in our words alone.

When God first gave me the basis for my blessings teaching in 2004, I received a whole new perspective on how we can intentionally open doors of blessing for others and *target* them for good.

It was a rainy spring afternoon in the Pacific Northwest when I found myself, yet again, standing in line at my local post office. I am a people watcher, and the post office was packed that particular day. I had a lot to keep me occupied while I waited. A lady began to sneeze, quickly drawing my attention. *Poor woman,* I thought, *she must be getting sick.* Then to my surprise, the postal worker waiting on her said, "God Bless You!" He proceeded to repeat this every time she sneezed.

Can he do that?! I thought. *Won't he get into trouble? Especially since we live in a day and time that doesn't allow a mix of God and government.*

As I pondered this interaction, God began to show me that when we speak well-meaning, well-intended words over others, it opens spiritual doors in their lives, allowing the Holy Spirit to *target* them for good. Even if they don't yet know the Lord, our words can be the very thing that opens them up to receive Holy Spirit arrows of blessings.

But wait, there's more.

Over the years, as I have taught the power of speaking prophetic blessings, God has shown me new and added layers. Yes, we can speak words of blessing over others, but how much more powerful would it be if we crafted prayers of blessing for our families, businesses, finances, churches, cities, states, and our nation? What if we intentionally sought the heart of God for these individuals, organizations, and places? Then simply and carefully fashioned our words in the form of a prophetic blessing or prayer. What if we wrote intentional, life-giving words over these people, places, things, and then chose to continually speak those words into the atmosphere?

With God, I have learned there is always more!

Have you ever noticed how certain cultures and people groups speak to their young children? Take the Jewish momma, for example. Have you ever listened to how they talk to their kids about their future? They are going to be the best … the brightest in their fields. They are going to be doctors and lawyers. They will grow up and change the world just by being in it. And you know what? They do. The kids believe what their parents and grandparents have spoken over them for years. Many grow up to do just what their momma spoke over them. Why? There is power in the spoken word, but even more, there is power in intentional blessing.

Blessings are a Biblical concept going back to the beginning when God created the heavens and the earth. They continued throughout the Scriptures from Genesis to Revelation and should continue today. You may be wondering what exactly constitutes a blessing or why they are important enough that we should be concerned with them today. Simply put, a blessing is a prayer or a request asking for God's special favor and protection to rest upon us or other people we bless. Blessings infuse people with hope in the present moment for a blessed future.

The spiritual gift of prophecy is designed to edify, exhort, and build up the body of Christ but it is and can be so much more than that. It is a safe way to open the door for God to show His kindness to those in need of Him. By pronouncing a blessing, you release the Holy Spirit to impact the lives of those around you for good. Our declaration not only releases God's intentions for others but also releases blessings to us. We can't out-give God, nor can we out bless Him.

> *Give, and you will receive. Your gift will return to you in full—pressed down, shaken together to make room for more, running over, and poured into your lap. The amount you give will determine the amount you get back.*
>
> Luke 6:38 NLT

When we speak words of blessing to others, we are a gift, and we are imparting gifts in the form of words fashioned as blessings.

> *... you will be a blessing. I will bless those who bless you ...*
>
> Genesis 12:2b-3a NIV

Not only are we a blessing, aka a gift, but God will bless those who bless us. This means, as we bless others, His blessing will be returned to us as well. By hearing what Heaven has to say about our children, our grandchildren, or even those we meet, we can impart a Kingdom Legacy. A Kingdom Legacy is about focusing on what will endure past our earthly lifetime. It's about living intentionally, speaking intentionally, and building intentionally for future generations, far outliving us in this lifetime. A Kingdom Legacy is the best gift we can give others.

The act of imparting blessings to future generations was first laid out in the Bible. Somehow over time, we lost this beautiful practice. I say it's time we grab hold of the Spiritual truths found in the Bible and bring them into the 21st century and beyond.

I want to leave a legacy for my children and my children's children. I desire to leave both a natural and a spiritual inheritance for them, imparting the truths I have gained from my years of walking with the Lord. I want to leave behind an inheritance that helps them start ahead of where I started. I want to teach and equip them with how to walk in spiritual truths and pass them along to future generations. I can only assume you do as well.

After all, isn't that why you picked up this book? To leave a legacy and relearn the lost art and the importance of blessing.

Rabbi Isaiah Rothstein, in his article, *The Power of the Jewish Blessings,* states: "More than mere expressions of gratitude, blessings are portals to other spiritual realms."[1] He goes on to explain that blessings are portals to the infinite. In the Torah, they are viewed as a conduit for potential, the spiritual and the physical. Yet, in our human nature, we forget this tradition today, for most who practice them have become rote through recitation.

In the Talmud[2] it states a person is obligated to recite one hundred blessings a day taken from Deuteronomy 10:12. There are blessings over food and drink, upon leaving the bathroom, before going to sleep, and during life cycle events.[3] Rabbi Rothstein goes on to discuss how in Jewish tradition, it is forbidden to benefit from the world without pronouncing a blessing. Reciting one hundred blessings a day is a way to live connected to the divine by living an immersed life of blessings and gratitude. Rabbi Rothstein poses an essential question regarding the blessing; "How do we make blessings more transformative rather than transactional?"[4]

Excellent question. His suggestion for those reading the article was to first meditate on each of the blessings recited and seek to understand their personal meaning. Rabbi Rothstein felt that by meditating on each blessing there would be transformation. Meditating on the meaning would change the person instead of treating the blessing as a recitation of a transaction, a box to check for daily obligations. Rothstein suggests we should become the blessing.

However, I want to take it one step further. I feel part of what we have lost in speaking blessings is their prophetic nature. Yes, reading the blessings of God in the Bible and pronouncing them over our lives and the lives of others is incredibly good. But what if we seek God and inquire what He would like us to impart to our children and our children's children? This kind of blessing would be an important, rich legacy for all God's family, Jew and Gentile alike, receiving the full benefit and power imparted.

> A blessing from God is a gift intended for our eternal benefit or good. A genuine blessing always has an eternal component.
>
> Dr. Charles Stanley[5]

Legacy Builders

Prayer

Father God, I want to not only be a blessing to others but also to impart blessings. Open my heart, spiritual eyes, and ears to hear clearly from You. Show me times when I have used my words to bring death, not life. I repent and ask You to forgive me for these times, and I receive Your forgiveness. Allow the words of my mouth to be life-giving and edifying to those I speak with and even when I speak about myself. Reveal how You see me and allow me to receive that truth. Impart truth to me and allow me to not just see in others what is already visible but to see the buried gold. God, I ask that you release your Holy Spirit to help me be a conduit for blessing others.

God, I strive to love you with my whole being as Your Word commands; help me where I am lacking. Also, help me love others well, not just in my actions, but with my words. Show me Your heart for others and help me to see in them what You see. I ask all this in the mighty name of Your son Jesus, Amen!

Reflection

What are your thoughts regarding blessings?

What kind of legacy do you want to leave for others?

How can you make blessings more transformative rather than transactional?

Blessing in Action

Think of someone you would like to encourage and speak a blessing to today. Once you have their name, ask God for a Scripture or kind words to speak over that individual as a blessing. Then write it out. Once you have the written kind word or Scripture, speak the blessing over them either in person or over the phone.

Chapter 2
The Power of Spoken Words

Reckless words pierce like a sword,
but the tongue of the wise brings healing.
Proverbs 12:18 NIV

As a young kid on the playground at school, when someone would say something unkind, my friends and I would chant in a sing-song voice, "Sticks and stones may break my bones, but words will never hurt me." Wow, has there ever been a more delusional statement? While damaged and hurt, my body can heal from broken bones and physical bruises. However, the harm words can do goes much deeper and can cause years of emotional trauma and pain.

There is a compelling image of the power of our words I like to show when teaching about the effect they have on kids. Maybe you've seen it before? It's a picture of a young boy with sad big brown eyes. A hand encircles his throat as if choking him. The hand is made up of words—negative words, that is. Words meant to hurt and harm—words intended to inflict pain when spoken. When we voice negative, harsh, and harmful words like this, it's as if we're strangling or suffocating the individual. The image is powerful and makes me stop to think about the words I speak. Most of us don't purposefully express negative words, yet they slip out. Whether intentional or unintentional, they shift and change things once they are released into the atmosphere. Negative words affect the environment around us and the feelings within us. When someone speaks harsh words to us, we are affected by them even if we don't acknowledge them. Words are like seeds planted in the ground, except they're sowed into hearts and minds. Be careful what you speak. Guard your heart and mind, for out of the abundance of the heart, the mouth speaks (see Matthew 12:34; Luke 6:45).

Years ago, when I took a healing class called *"Cleansing Stream,"* they used a visual example of what it's like when we attempt to retract words that have already been spoken. Take a tube of toothpaste, for example. If an excess amount of toothpaste is squeezed out of the tube, no amount of trying can get the extra back into the tube. Once it has been squeezed out, it's out for good. I know. I've tried, but it only made a bigger mess. The same is true of our words. Once you speak them, no matter how hard you try, you cannot get them back or pretend they were never said.

I teach in-depth about the power of our tongue and the importance of renewing our minds in my training manual, *Releasing God's Heart through Hearing His Voice.* So, for those who have already read or heard some of this, I apologize, but it bears repeating. When I teach classes in person or online, I want to lay a solid Biblical foundation for individuals as they begin to hear from God for themselves and minister to others. I believe learning to control and tame our tongue, as one translation says, is of the utmost importance.

Why is it important?

What's so important and why do our words matter? First, I encourage you to read James 3 in its entirety to get the fullest picture possible. However, if we start at the beginning, we see the power of the spoken word. Genesis 1:26 tells us we are created in the image of God. When God spoke, He did so with authority and power. When He spoke, things were created and came into being. He spoke and it simply was. Because we are made in His image, our tongue, and the words we speak are powerful and can be used for good or evil. They can bring life or death (see James 3:9-10 and Proverbs 18:26).

But that's not all. We are designed to listen to what's spoken to us by others and even what we speak or think about ourselves. In Romans 12, Paul talks about the importance of renewing our minds. Many of us have negative sound bites or "tapes" playing over and over in our minds, affecting how we live today. Sounds bites like, *you're never going to amount to anything, you're too young or too old.* Sometimes we can even get stuck always looking back at the past reliving or replaying our glory days. There's an unbreakable link between our thoughts, actions, and speech. Just as the rudder of a ship directs the entire ship, our tongue directs the course of our life. What you say matters. If you look for the worst and speak the negative, you will often find it. For example, perhaps you're dreading a meeting with your boss and talk about how terrible it's going to be. In all likelihood, it will become a self-fulfilling prophecy and turn out just the way you thought it would. We need to replace these negative tapes with positive sound bites. Speak Scripture out loud to transform your mind. Instead of dreading meeting with your boss and expecting the worst, speak this instead: Just as both Samuel and Jesus grew in favor with God and man (see 1 Samuel 2:26; Luke 2:52), I will too, especially at work. This is part of renewing and restoring your mind as Paul instructs us.

> *Do not conform to the pattern of this world, but be transformed by the renewing of your mind.*
> Romans 12:2a NIV

With our tongue, we form words, which can be powerful life-giving blessings or lethal weapons of destruction. The choice is ours.

> *Out of the abundance of the heart, the mouth speaks.*
> Luke 6:45 NIV

In his book, *The Power of the Blessings*, Kerry Kirkwood shares the story of Marcus,[6] who became a house painter. When asked why he chose to become a painter, Marcus relays the story of his childhood and how his father never praised him for being good at anything. That is, except once. Marcus's father was a traveling salesman and one time when he came home from a business trip, Marcus was painting a birdhouse he had made at school. When his father saw this, he commented on what a good painter he was. These words spoken by Marcus's father were some of the only affirming comments his dad ever made to him. It's no surprise Marcus became a house painter since he believed it was the only thing he was good at.

> *For as he thinketh in his heart, so is he.*
> Proverbs 23:7 KJV

Our heart and our brain are connected. That's also why we're instructed to take every thought captive and make it obedient to Christ (2 Corinthians 10:3-6). "It is imperative that we examine our speech and guard the words of our mouth. This is a significant key in mind renewal. Find the truth in Scripture and use it to renew your mind. We are new creations in Christ– recognize the authority of your voice and use it wisely."[7] Use your words wisely to leave a Godly legacy not just for you and your family but to deposit seeds of blessings to facilitate the legacy of others as well.

Our words not only direct our life and set us on a course for thriving or destruction, but our words can change the atmosphere around us for positive or negative. We've all known people whom we may consider to be "Debbie downers". They're the glass is half-empty types. The negative side of every situation always comes out of their mouth. It's as if they aren't just looking for something bad to happen, they expect it to. Their fears, doubts, and insecurities flow unchecked. Instead of speaking with hope and life, they put a damper on situations. Conversely, there are the glass is half-full individuals. They are always overjoyed to share the endless possibilities of all that can go right. You speak a negative and they counter it with a positive. You share a fear or concern, they share hope and a solution. If life gives them a lemon, they make lemonade. Think of it this way, with a classic example from Winnie the Pooh. Eeyore is always sad, down, and wondering why anyone ever bothers. In fact, his famous line is, "Oh bother" with a deep sigh of discouragement in his voice. Then there is Tigger (he's my favorite) who is always energetic and looking for fun in everything. He's always pushing Eeyore to explore more, have fun, and be more adventurous, and just so you know, the Holy Spirit is just like Tigger in many ways!

> *Those who guard their mouths and their tongues*
> *keeps themselves from calamity.*
> Proverbs 21:23 NIV

It has been said that it takes thirty-seven positives to offset one negative in the heart of a child.[8] Yet when we become adults, we are not as resilient as we once were, so I believe that number is much higher.

Researchers continue to attempt to determine just how many positive interactions are needed to offset one negative interaction. They have created whole programs and protocols around such things. For example, in 2020, Psychology Today posted an online article discussing the "3-To-1 Positivity Ratio."

> According to Dr. Barbara Fredrickson, a positivity researcher at the University of North Carolina, for every heart-wrenching negative emotional experience you endure, you need to experience at least three heartfelt positive emotional experiences that uplift you.[9]

There is also the "5-to-1 Ratio," which is used in schools. A 2021 article from "Education and Behavior" online states:

> Research supports the idea that having five positive interactions to every one negative interaction best supports and sustains constructive student-teacher relationships. This is known as the 5-to-1 ratio. The 5-to-1 ratio is meant to improve students' feelings of connectedness and positivity in order to facilitate the classroom experience. The 5-to-1 ratio can improve academic engagement and reduce classroom disruptions, simply because the classroom has a more positive climate.
>
> Creating positive interactions in the classroom helps students invest in the value and purpose of classroom instruction."[10]

Finally, in a 2008 *Today's Christian Woman,* there was an article discussing how our brains need more positive interactions to counteract our negative biases. However, it went on to say:

> Not only do we have a built-in partiality toward negative information, but negatives increase disproportionately over positives. It's not a one-to-one ratio. In other words, one positive cannot offset one negative. When you tell your husband, "Thanks for giving the kids a bath, honey," and five minutes later say, "You forgot to take out the trash—again," the negative drowns out the positive.

Our brain needs a higher number of positive entries to counterbalance this built-in negativity bias. And several small, frequent, positive acts pack more punch than one giant-size positive. The size of the positive doesn't count; quantity does. It's strictly a numbers game. ... One super-size positive cannot offset multiple negatives.[11]

Exactly how many positives are needed to offset one negative? What works for one person may not work for someone else. We all have negative biases and a built-in tolerance regarding how much we can take. The same *Today's Christian Woman* article as above from 2008 said:

At least two-to-one, experts say. Researchers have concluded that when applying this formula to our most intimate relationships, the ratio of positives must be even higher. Among those researchers is psychologist Dr. John Gottman at the University of Washington. Gottman says the formula should be five-to-one for married couples.[12]

The bottom line is this: Words are *powerful*. Choose them wisely. Be careful when you speak, be careful how you speak, and do your best not to use your words to harm others. We must give an account of every idle word we speak in our lifetime. Our tongue is such a vital part of our make-up. Scripture says that the power of life and death is in the tongue (Proverbs 18:21).

But I tell you that everyone will have to give account on the day of judgment for every careless word they have spoken. For by your words you will be acquitted, and by your words, you will be condemned.

Matthew 12:36-37 NIV

Bill Gothard, in his book *The Power of Spoken Blessing*, says:

Our words have lasting impact not only for harm, but also for great good. By speaking blessings, we can help bring healing to aching souls and restoration to bruised relationships. [13]

Let's choose to be a positive force in someone's life today! It's really easy and can be a lot of fun. I will discuss more in later chapters on how to intentionally speak a blessing to someone by speaking a well-meaning, well-intended word over them and their future.

> *But encourage one another **day after day**, as long as it is still called "**Today**," so that none of you will be hardened by the deceitfulness of sin.*
> Hebrews 3:13 NASB

Words Matter

I hate to break it to you, but that old nursery school rhyme, *Sticks and Stones*, is a lie. Words have power, but even more than that, they carry a certain weight and authority. Whether you believe in Christ or not, there is enough scientific research to back up just how powerful words can be. The words we speak and how we speak them matter.

In an online article from 2017 by Andrew Wilinski about choosing words wisely, he quotes author Yehuda Berg who states:

> Words are singularly the most powerful force available to humanity… Words have energy and power with the ability to help, to heal, to hurt, to harm, to humiliate, and to humble. [14]

Now, I am not recommending you read his books, because his beliefs don't align with the Christian faith, but I find it profound that the world understands the importance and power of spoken words sometimes more than I think the church does. In my book, *Releasing God's Heart through Hearing His Voice*, I stated this concerning the power of our words.

> Words have authority in the spirit realm. When you voice your thoughts or opinions, you are speaking or giving authority to one side or another. In Genesis 1, several verses tell us God spoke and something was created. When God spoke, He used words. The Scriptures do not say God laid His

hands on particles or that He got out His spiritual hammer and nails and went to work. It states simply, "God spoke" and it was! Genesis also states that we are created in His image (Genesis 1:26). Since we are made in His image, then we too have been given authority when we speak. How are you using your authority?[15]

In his online article, Wilinski discusses how words can make a difference in our life and the world. He says:

Words. Are. Powerful. Think of powerful words throughout history which have had a lasting difference in our world. "Four score and seven years ago." "I have a dream." "Tear down this wall." Our words, when chosen correctly, can make a positive contribution in our own lives and the lives of those around us.

Words filter through us and seep into our community, where they are absorbed then reasserted by others to people they know. When we recognize the power our words have, we see the impact they can have and we choose them based on what kind of difference we want to make.[16]

The words of the reckless pierce like swords, but the tongue of the wise brings healing.
Proverbs 12:18 NIV

A man's self will be filled with the fruit of his mouth.
Proverbs 18:20 AMPC

Power of Words

In his book, *Messages from Water*, Dr. Masaru Emoto shares his idea that the molecular structure of water is changed by words in the atmosphere or thoughts surrounding it. He conducted several experiments showing how water's molecular structure can be altered. Some claim his hypothesis to be baseless and his experiments lack credibility. However, as I have read the book and watched YouTube videos with interviews and images of his research and what he discovered, I am a believer. Not necessarily in the science or his research, but in how God created things to function. Let me expound. The human body is made up of 50-75% water.[17] Dr. Emoto explains his experiments and theory that words spoken, and even emotions in the atmosphere, can change the molecular make-up of the water. Water that has a good atmosphere around it or words of affirmation, blessing, or love spoken over it will produce beautiful, clear, pristine-looking crystals under a microscope. On the other side, water which is surrounded by a lot of negativity, anger, and hate spoken into the atmosphere, produces malformed, dirty crystals under the microscope. If our bodies are made up of a good percentage of water, and we are saturated in a negative atmosphere, with many negative words, it will affect not just our brains and attitudes, but our physical body as well. The influence of negativity is far more damaging than we might realize.

Through many of the healing trainings and a variety of healing modalities I have studied, the scientific research easily establishes connections between trauma and the resulting memories being stored in our bodies and minds. Dr. Aiko Hormann[18] was one such person who studied this phenomenon. Dr. Aiko[19] came to the U.S. from Japan in 1951 and earned her degree in mathematics at the University of Missouri. Hormann became a research scientist specializing in artificial intelligence and the human brain. In 1968, Hormann became a Christian and started ministering and teaching on various subjects around inner healing to help individuals realize the fullness of the potential God has put within them.

Another healing modality I've been trained in is Healing Timeline.[20] The idea of this modality is that traumatic memories are stored in the timeline of our life. For example, when a tree is cut down, you can tell by its inner rings when trauma like fire, droughts, and floods have occurred. Our memories serve as the "rings of a tree" in our timeline of life.

My dad was a logger, and I grew up going with him to job sites and even worked as a choker setter for him during the summer. A choker setter is someone who attaches cables to logs for retrieval. Once after cutting down a rather large tree, my dad called my sister and I over to look at the tree's life story. He told us how old the tree was by counting its rings and even pointed out the times in its life when things looked "healthy" and normal and other times when there had been a fire or lack of water. I was intrigued that I could uncover the history of a tree's life just by looking at the rings of a stump that was left behind. So, when I took the training for the healing timeline modality, it was easy to connect the "trauma" that occurs in our life and understand how our mind and body store it. This made it easy to accept Dr. Emoto's ideas and theory around water as well.

Not only is the power of words a concept I have read about, but I also teach on it, and I have also experienced it in my own life. In my book, *Releasing God's Heart: Through Hearing His Voice,* I share it this way: "We are designed to listen to what we say about ourselves and what others say about us. That is why it is so important that we guard our words. Our tongue and the words of our mouth are powerful weapons that can be used either for good or evil (see James 3:9-10). We can bring life or death by simply speaking."[21] We can use our words to speak life or death over ourselves, others, situations, and even other living creatures.

Our family learned this lesson the hard way. Before I share this with you and you think my husband is a terrible person, I assure you, he is not. However, he definitely had an issue with our dog, Sophie. Though it was actually Sophie who was the problem … she hated people. She thought she was a hundred-pound rottweiler but she was a five-and-a-half-pound tea-cup Maltese. Everyone who knew Sophie would joke, "she was possessed." In actuality, she was stuck in the birth canal, deprived of oxygen, but was later resuscitated.

I use this as my reasoning when defending her psychotic episodes and erratic behavior. Just to help you understand, let me give you a small glimpse into why John reacted the way he did to Sophie. When people would visit, she would run underneath the couch and growl and bark incessantly. Then, as our guests walked across the room, down the hallway, or were preparing to leave, she would charge from underneath the couch and bite their pantlegs, snarling and growling the entire time. The only person she didn't really do that to was me, but she would even try to take a nip out of me every now and then.

One particular evening, John and I were getting ready for bed. I was reading, with Sophie lying beside me on the bed. John walked into the room, and she went berserk. She got up and charged to the end of the bed with teeth barred, barking and growling. John pointed his finger at her and emphatically said, "Why don't you get sick and die!" I, of course, calmed

Sophie down and told John he wasn't being nice and to stop speaking to her like that. Neither of us gave it much thought until a few days later. Sophie began doing strange things like staring at the hallway wall and barking at nothing for no apparent reason. She began to cough and act stranger than usual. While we went on vacation and one of our friends came over to house/pet sit. During our time away, she called a few times to tell me Sophie didn't seem to be doing too well and didn't want her to "die" on her watch. I assured her she could take her to the vet if needed and that I wouldn't blame her if something happened.

When we returned from vacation, Sophie was worse. She acted like she had a cold. She was coughing, sneezing, and wheezing, not to mention randomly barking at walls and emptily staring at nothing. The vet didn't find anything wrong with her when I took her in but she seemed to get worse later that day. That night, I laid my hands on her, prayed, and asked God for wisdom. It was too late to call the vet again, but I planned to in the morning. It was then that the Holy Spirit brought back to memory the "curse" John spoke over her before we left. I immediately went to him and demanded he lay hands on Sophie, pray for her healing, bless her, and break the word curse he had spoken! He grumbled and complained, but in the end, he had a change of heart and did just that. By the next morning, Sophie was acting better and within a day or so, she was no longer coughing, wheezing, or acting oddly. John had spoken a curse of death over the dog, and he needed to release a blessing to break the curse he had spoken. Once he did, Sophie turned around. I would like to say she stopped running under the couch barking and attacking people's pant legs, but she didn't, bless her heart.

While the story is about an animal and we think we'd never speak a curse like that over an individual, the truth is, we can do just as much damage with our words and speak curses that have the same effect. We must choose to speak life! The enemy gains power when we come into agreement with the thoughts and lies he whispers to us. But when we come in agreement with God and His Kingdom principles, everything shifts and changes. When we align our speech with Scripture, the very heart of the Father, we can use our prophetic voice to shift atmospheres. Not only that, we can decree, declare, and establish things God shows us in the natural. A blessing pronounced is a prophetic word and we can prophesy by speaking a blessing to others.

Our prophetic voice can bring forth blessings in the name of Jesus. We can impart powerful spoken blessings to our family, other individuals, and even over our own life. Pronouncing a blessing opens the door for God to show His kindness. Speaking a deliberate blessing/statement opens a spiritual door for the Holy Spirit to impact lives.

Legacy Builders

Prayer

God, I repent of any time I have spoken reckless words causing damage to myself or anyone else. Forgive me for not fully understanding the power of my words. I now recognize my words have power and authority and only want to use them to bring about life and blessing. Remove and break any legal right I may have given the enemy through my spoken words. Break them not just over my life but in the lives of others. Place a guard over my mouth and keep my tongue from lashing out. Fill my heart with love, praise, and blessings so they may overflow my mouth. Please fill me with your wisdom and allow my tongue to bring healing. Amen!

Reflection

As you look back over the "timeline" of your life, might there be places where words created trauma still affecting you today? If so, seek the Holy Spirit as to how to best deal with it. (You can pray and ask Him to bring healing and take it out at the root. However, in some cases, you may need to schedule an appointment with someone who can walk you through healing).

What direction for your life have your words been setting?

How can you be a positive force in someone's life today?

Blessing in Action

Ask the Holy Spirit to reveal a lie you believe about yourself or negative words of death you have spoken over yourself. Once He has shown you the lie or the negative words, ask Him to reveal the truth to you. Once He shows you the truth, write it out so you can speak it out loud over yourself daily. Then take it one step further: Find a Scripture that aligns with this truth and meditate on it daily as well.

Example:
Lie: I am unlovable
Truth: God loves me
Scripture: John 15:12-13; John 3:16; Romans 5:5; 1 John 4:19-21; Psalm 139:14-16

Chapter 3
What is a Blessing?

So they will put my name on the Israelites, and I
will bless them.

Numbers 6:27 NIV

A blessing is an act of declaring favor and goodness upon others. A Biblical blessing is one way of asking for God's divine favor to rest upon others.

The most famous blessing of the Bible is found in Numbers 6:22-27 which we will talk more about in a later chapter. I am sure you have heard these verses quoted as benedictions in part or their entirety.

The LORD bless you
and keep you;
the LORD make his face shine on you
and be gracious to you;
the LORD turn his face toward you
and give you peace.

Numbers 24-26 NIV

This blessing from Numbers 6 is a perfect example of how blessings are powerful, life-giving, and prophetic in nature.

To better understand what a blessing is, it's important to have an accurate definition. The dictionary says this about blessings:

Bless (blĕs) *tr.v.* blessed, or blest (blĕst) bless·ing, bless·es
1. To make holy by religious rite; sanctify.
2. To make the sign of the cross over so as to sanctify.
3. To invoke divine favor upon.
4. To honor as holy; glorify: *Bless the Lord.*
5. To confer well-being or prosperity on.
6. To endow, as with talent.

And the word *blessings* in Greek is: **eulogeo** (yoo-log-eh'o) Bless
1. To pronounce a blessing on
2. Favored of God
3. To cause to prosper, to make happy, to bestow blessings upon

eneulogeo – en-you-log-eh'o blessed
1. To confer benefits on – to bless

English - **Eulogy** – speech in praise or some person or something – High praise.

Our English word is made up of two words in the Greek.
1. **eu** – meaning well
2. **logo**s – meaning word

Translators used the Greek word eulogy to translate the Hebrew word *bless*. In the Old Testament, the word for *bless* is **barak** and appears 330 times.

The Definition of Barak[22] is:
1. to bless, kneel
   a. (Niphal) to be blessed, bless oneself
   b. (Piel) to bless
   c. (Pual) to be blessed, be adored
   d. (Hiphil) to cause to kneel
   e. (Hithpael) to bless oneself
2. (TWOT) to praise, salute, curse

In the New Testament, the word for *bless* is **eulogeo** and, in its many other forms, appears forty-four times.

Definition of eulogeō[23] is:

1. to praise, celebrate with praises
2. to invoke blessings
3. to consecrate a thing with solemn prayers
   a. to ask God's blessing on a thing
   b. pray God to bless it to one's use
   c. pronounce a consecratory blessing on
4. of God
   a. to cause to prosper, to make happy, to bestow blessings on
   b. favored of God, blessed

I always say it's important if it's in the Word of God. But if it's repeated more than once, we had better pay attention because there is a significant spiritual key or concept God is trying to convey. This is the case with the concept of blessings. It's a concept that is repeated many times over.

The Theory of Repetition

I have this theory that I call the "theory of repetition." The theory is simple: Pay attention to repeated themes, words, and concepts... not just in Scripture, but also in everyday life. When we see repetition, there is usually an important message or concept attached for us. How do we figure out what the message or concept is? Simple. We must ask God questions and be open to hearing His response.

Of course, we can see themes throughout Scripture and understand their importance but there is always a deeper level of revelation and understanding to be had. Did you know the word *love*, in all its different forms and meanings, is used over 500 times throughout the Bible, depending on which version/translation you use? Our English word for love is not as comprehensive as the Greek words for love. We English-speaking individuals use the word *love* to talk about food we favor, television shows we watch, and even to describe how we feel about people we're in relationship with. However, in the Bible, the Greek word love is broken down into different kinds of love: storge love, phileo love, eros love and agape love.

The four kinds of love are:
- Storge – empathy bond.
- Phileo – friend bond.
- Eros – romantic love.
- Agape – unconditional "God" love.

Let's look at the story of Jesus restoring Peter after he had denied Christ three times. Again, we see more repetition. As if denying Christ once wasn't enough, Peter denied Him three times. Why? Well, first Jesus told Peter he would deny Him three times. But there is an importance to why it happened more than once. Don't just take my word for it, take some time to ask the Holy Spirit yourself to see what He has to say about the importance of the three denials.

When Jesus restored Peter, he repeatedly asked him the same question: "Peter, do you love me?" (see John 21:15-1). And Peter always responded, "Yes, I love you." After several of these question-and-answer cycles, Jesus finally commanded Peter to "feed His sheep". I have heard many a preacher say Jesus asked the same question three times to offset the number of times Peter had denied him. In doing so, Peter was restored. But I believe there is more to the story than what we see or read on the surface.

I believe one of the reasons is rooted in the use of the word "love". If you read the Bible without looking at the original Greek language, you will miss the subtleties of what Christ was doing … as well as the meaning of Peter's response. The word *love* in the English language is not as rich, deep, or meaningful as the varying types of love in Greek, as I explained before.

So, what does all this have to do with Peter's restoration? You don't need the fancy logos Bible software to discover the answer, although it does make research easier. All you really need is blueletterbible.com or even a hard copy of a Strong's Concordance and your Bible.

As you read the account in John 21:15-17, Jesus asks Peter, "Do you love me?" Christ's use of the word *love* is the Greek word, *Agape*. *Agape* love is an unconditional God kind of love. Peter's response, however, was not "Yes, Lord. You know I *agape* love You." No, Peter's answer was the Greek word *phileo,* the brotherly, friend kind of love. The conversation went like this twice:

Jesus asks Peter, "Do you *agape* me?
Peter responds, "Yes, Lord. You know I *phileo* You."
Then it gets interesting because the third time Jesus questions Peter, he switches meaning. "Do you *phileo* me?" Jesus came to Peter's level and instead of using the word agape, as He did twice before, He used the word *phileo*.

Jesus matched Peter's sentiment, but why? Again, another great question to ask the Holy Spirit about. But here are some of my thoughts:

Jesus was calling Peter up to a higher level of leadership. Once Christ returned to Heaven, He knew God's plans for Peter. Peter would take a key role in leading the growing Church of Christ and spreading the Gospel. To do that, Peter would need to be stretched beyond just the *phileo*, brotherly love. Peter would need to understand the agape, unconditional God kind of love.

Another reason for the repetitive questioning by Christ is that He needed Peter to understand what Jesus was asking and tasking him with was extremely important. It wasn't just important, "Hey, Peter, feed my sheep." It was essential!

When a parent, a boss, or someone else repeats themselves more than once, it triggers something in our brains telling us, this isn't just information and kind of important, it is extremely important. Whether it be instruction or a casual conversation, when we hear someone repeat something, we listen more carefully and intentionally.

I know as a wife and parent that if I want my husband or kids to hear what I'm saying, I'll likely have to repeat myself. When having any discussion with my family, they know that if I do that, it's because what I am saying is important. When I preach or teach, I will repeat certain things because they are important and valuable.

God does the same thing. Much of Scripture has a repetitive nature to it. There are parallel messages and themes between the Old and New Testaments. God is in the business of repeating himself, not just because we are hard of hearing, but because we often miss the importance of something the first time around.

I came up with my "theory of repetition" when I first learned and understood how to hear God. I grew up not realizing God wanted a real relationship with a two-way conversation! I had to learn He was speaking all the time and wanted to speak to me. I needed to understand I could speak to God, and He would respond. I also used to think I was a little on the slow or dull side because God would have to convey His message to me in various ways before I would actually "get it."

For example, one day I was at the local Staples making copies for my boss because our small office printer was broken. I had a bad attitude and was leading a rather one-way, heated conversation with God in my mind. I don't recall what I had been praying about but I didn't like His silence. I am sure all the "why questions" were involved and I was having a full-blown pity party.

Prior to arriving at Staples, I happened to cross paths with two people who were disabled and didn't give either one a second thought. After finishing making copies and heading for the door, a man on crutches walked toward me. I glanced down to see why he was on crutches. Did he have a broken foot? A bum knee? Or something else? It was definitely something else. He had one leg amputated and the other was a prosthetic peg leg.

Not what I expected, but since this was the third disabled person in a matter of thirty minutes, I knew there was a message in it for me. I promise I am not in the habit of over-spiritualizing things. I do not look for a demon behind every rock, nor do I ask God to speak about every minor detail of my life, like what I should wear today or what food I should eat for each meal. Do I have an ongoing conversation with Him? Yes. But I figure we have more important things to discuss than wearing a black or pink shirt.

I can hear you asking: What was the message? Why would God use people with missing body parts to speak to you? The basic message was that my attitude was a hindrance and was disabling my forward motion. It perfectly addressed the lousy attitude and pathetic pity party I had just had moments before.

Sometimes God repeats messages and concepts not just so we hear them but to make sure we understand their importance. He wants us to pay attention and dig for deeper meaning and understanding. God arranged multiple situations where I encountered disabled people so He could get His message across to me. When I didn't get it the first time, so he had to repeat himself, much like Jesus did when He asked Peter if he loved Him three times.

And so it is with blessings. When we look at the many times they are mentioned in Scripture, we can see it's a concept and topic that's important to the Lord. Yet today, blessings are not readily pronounced unless perhaps you're at a wedding, a baby shower, or a baby dedication. We don't often hear of an ailing patriarch/matriarch of the family gathering family members towards the end of their life and pronouncing blessings over them before they pass, as we see modeled in Scripture. They aren't really prevalent in our society or culture.

According to the definition and commentary regarding "Blessing" in Baker's Evangelical Dictionary of Theology,[24] a blessing is:

> God's intention and desire to bless humanity is a central focus of his covenant relationships. For this reason, the concept of blessing pervades the biblical record. Two distinct ideas are present. First, a blessing was a public declaration of a favored status with God. Second, the blessing endowed power for prosperity and success. In all cases, the blessing served as a guide and motivation to pursue a course of life within the blessing.

Here are some of the different themes and kinds of blessings throughout Scripture that emerge when you begin to research them:

First, they are spoken to invoke God's blessing on another individual.

> *May God Almighty bless you and make you fruitful and increase your numbers until you become a community of peoples. May he give you and your descendants the blessing given to Abraham, so that you may take possession of the land where you now reside as a foreigner, the land God gave to Abraham.*
>
> Genesis 28:3-4 NIV

Next, Deuteronomy 28 talks in depth about the blessings of obedience and curses of disobedience. But it also states blessings are a sign of favor and are intended to result in success and prosperity (see Deuteronomy 28:3-7).

Then there are the blessings we see in the Old Testament where someone greater blesses someone lesser. Such as a father passing down a blessing to his children as Isaac did with Jacob and Esau (see Genesis 27). Jacob blessed Joseph (see Genesis 49:22-26), and Joseph also brought his children, Ephraim and Manasseh, to Jacob so he could release a patriarchal and grandfatherly blessing over them (see Genesis 48). We also see the writer of the book of Hebrews confirm this type of blessing when we read of Melchizedek's being the greater over Abraham and pronouncing a blessing upon him (see Hebrews 7:6-7).

In Scripture, there are other places where general blessings are spoken and imparted to the righteous.[25] But blessings are not always toward individuals. We can also bless God through our worship, words, and praise. The Psalms are full of places where David praises and blesses God for who He is and what He has done.

> *"Bless the Lord, O my soul, and forget not all his benefits."*
>
> Psalm 103:2 KJV

The Baker's Evangelical Dictionary of Theology states that "the parallels between the Old and New Testament usages of blessing are striking. To be blessed is to be granted special favor by God with resulting joy and prosperity. In the New Testament, the emphasis is more on spiritual rather than on material blessings."[26]

I found the last statement to be the opposite in today's current societal conditions. I will share more on this in a later chapter, but suffice it to say, the emphasis today is more on material blessing rather than spiritual, which saddens me. However, we can affect change in this area as we begin to "change the world one word at a time." If you've read my other books, but especially, *The Gift of Prophetic Encouragement: Hearing the Words of God for Others* (Chosen Books, 2018), you know this is a common phrase I coined and even put on t-shirts. Yes, we can "Change the World!" It is not meant to be a daunting task, as one of my friends and launch team members stated when she first saw my t-shirt. She called me to tell me she didn't like the words I had chosen to use as a hashtag and on my promotional materials. She told me it felt like a heavy burden and daunting task. I heard her out and asked if I could share my heart and explain what I meant. She agreed.

I completely understood where she was coming from. Yes, changing the world all by ourselves can be a daunting task. However, we are not doing it alone. Not only do we partner with the Holy Spirit to be his hands, feet, and mouthpiece but if we all do our part to change the sphere of influence we walk in daily then we'll effect change in the whole world. When you do your part, I do my part, and others do theirs to speak words of hope, life, and love to others, it changes the atmosphere and the people we speak to. This affects change in their lives and their family's lives because we spoke words from God's perspective that shifted atmospheres.

Blessings are intentional, well-placed, spoken words. We can change our world and the lives (worlds) of others by releasing spiritual blessings. We have the opportunity to leave a lasting legacy for every person we meet by hearing from heaven, declaring God's goodness upon them, and asking for His favor to rest upon them. When they encounter a blessing, they are more able to be a blessing.

Legacy Builders

Prayer

Father, I want to be a blessing to others and bless them with my words. Show me how to partner with the Holy Spirit to speak words of life, hope, and love to those I meet. Impart the Spirit of Wisdom to me so I can fully understand the deeper things of God. Help me to see and hear things from a heavenly perspective so I can be an atmosphere changer. Holy Spirit, equip and empower me to change the world around me by speaking Your heart over situations and toward people. Amen.

Reflection

In your own words, define what a blessing is.

Looking back, have there been times in your life when God may have been trying to get your attention (like my Staples story), or has He had to repeat himself to you?

How can you speak blessings to be an atmosphere changer?

Blessing in Action

Ask God for the name of someone you can bless and declare His favor and goodness over today.

Chapter 4
A Living Eulogy

Do not let any unwholesome talk come out of your mouths, but only what is helpful for building others up according to their needs, that it may benefit those who listen.

Ephesians 4:29 NIV

When I was seventeen, my girlfriends and I made plans to go to a dance club in celebration of a friend's birthday and generally just be seniors in high school. My friends wanted me to drive because I had a car that would seat everyone. My parents on the other hand told me I couldn't go. I snuck off anyway and promptly got caught because my car was broken into. My brand new, expensive jacket I worked and saved months for, was stolen as well as my friend's jackets and some of their purses. I hate having something stolen or lost and I remember voicing my frustration about this after getting in trouble. Unfortunately, my dad made a habit out of turning the other cheek and wanted us to do the same. He had always been that way and this instance was no different. "Well, I guess they needed your jacket more than you did," he calmly replied to my complaint. *WHAT?!* I wanted to scream. Clearly, I was not going to get any sympathy from dad. He didn't see the injustice of the situation. I had worked hard for the money to purchase that jacket. They took it. Stealing wasn't working. It wasn't honest. It was thievery. "I guess the good Lord knew they needed it more than you?" was consistently his response in similar situations. Okay, I seriously doubted that, but this was dad's philosophy—skewed as it was.

Dad was a glass-half-full kinda guy. I get it. I am, too. I can always see the positive in things. To me though, it was a bit delusional to excuse stealing by thinking someone needed it more. My husband pointed out later that my dad's viewpoint was much sounder and more Scriptural than my own. I don't like to admit it, but he was right.

> *Give to everyone who begs from you, and from one*
> *who takes away your goods do not demand them*
> *back.*
>
> Luke 6:30 ESV

It wasn't until I was an adult with kids of my own that I began to really understand the "why" behind my dad's seemingly illogical line of thinking. I came to realize my dad felt what he worked so hard for was always for others. He was used to sacrificing his wishes, wants, and desires to that goal.

It started when he was a teenager. My dad's father died suddenly when he was a young teenager, and he was immediately thrust into being "the man" of the family. He became responsible for caring for his mother, two sisters, and a developmentally delayed brother. My grandmother worked, but the responsibilities of being the head of the household fell to my dad. He didn't talk much about growing up, but his family was very dysfunctional. I'm not sure my grandmother really knew the demands she put on my dad were too much for a teenager emotionally. Or at least I like to think she didn't fully understand the damage she did. And as a kid, I didn't see it either, but later in life, I could when looking back through the seasons of healing.

My dad was a wonderful, tender-hearted, generous, giving man. He would give the shirt off his back if needed. He would give the last dollar out of his wallet or the last coin in his pocket, even if it meant he didn't have two pennies to rub together. Everyone knew this and most respected him and blessed him for it. But there were always a few who took advantage of it too. Especially his siblings.

My dad's brother died when I was a teenager and my grandmother passed away suddenly a month before my oldest child was born. I watched my dad labor tirelessly to manage and ensure my grandmother's wishes were met concerning her estate. But when all the hard work was finished, my dad's sisters decided to sue him for the executorship of her estate together. Both aunts, who never really got along, decided to bury the hatchet and work together to force my dad out in order to split the remainder of the money. My dad, always the peacemaker with the "they must have needed it more," attitude just walked away from the fight. Truth be told, he had the legal system on his side, but his entire life had conditioned him not to fight. My aunts were out for themselves and focused on worldly possessions. My dad felt it wasn't worth the time, effort, or trouble to battle them. They were in our life for a year after my grandmother passed away, but after they got what they had sought, we never really heard from them again.

At my dad's memorial service, many people shared stories and memories about him. Some I had heard and others I hadn't. The common theme of my dad's life was his generosity, servanthood, and sense of humor.

It was my job to write dad's obituary, which my husband read at his memorial service. My brother-in-law, my son, and even my husband honored my dad and gave "eulogies" speaking of his character and who he was, as did many others.

Let's pause for a minute and think about when we typically hear or give a eulogy.

According to the dictionary, a eulogy is:
noun

1. a speech or piece of writing that praises some-one or something highly, typically someone who has just died."[27]
2. a commendatory oration or writing especially in honor of one deceased [28]
3. high praise[29]

When I was tasked with writing my dad's obituary, I googled things like: "How to write an obituary" and "What is the purpose of the eulogy?"

I found this explanation helpful regarding a eulogy:

A eulogy is a speech given at a memorial service in memory of a person who has died. The purpose is **to recall the defining qualities and highlights of a life lived in a way that benefits the audience, particularly the family**. It should capture the essence of the life lived.[30]

There it is … a eulogy "should capture the essence of the **life lived**." Traditionally a eulogy is given after a person has died. Even the dictionary definition tells us it is a speech or piece of writing honoring someone after they are deceased. But why don't we give a eulogy to capture life while it's being lived?

I find this very sad, don't you? Unfortunately, the only time we mention the good we see in people is after they have passed on and that good can no longer influence them. I wonder if we were to give living eulogies to the people in our lives, would it change things? I wonder if my dad realized what people valued and honored in him? I wonder if he knew how much he mattered to so many.

The Bible tells of two separate instances where individuals eulogized and anointed Jesus. One was Mary (see Matthew 26:6-13) and the other was Nicodemus (see John 19:38-40). One is remembered more than the other but why? Jesus even stated that Mary would be remembered for years to come for what she had done.

> *Assuredly, I say to you, wherever this gospel is preached in the whole world, what this woman has done will also be told as a memorial to her.*
> Matthew 26:13 NKJV

The simplicity of the matter is this: Mary anointed Jesus and spoke high praise of Him while He was alive, and Nicodemus honored and anointed Jesus after He was dead.

Dwight L Moody said it best:

> There is a lesson here. How very kind and thoughtful we are to a family who has lost some member, and what kind words are said after the person is dead and gone. Would it not be better to say a few of those good things before they go? Wouldn't it

be better to give some of your bouquets before a man dies and not go and load down his coffin with them? He cannot enjoy them then.[31]

So true! Mr. Moody hit the nail on the head; kind words after someone has passed from this life don't do them any good. However, what if we were to give living eulogies? What's a living eulogy, you ask? Speaking kind words and thoughts directly to a person so they can hear them, enjoy them, and even bask in them.

A Living Eulogy

For a person whose love language is words of affirmation, they seek to receive love through words spoken to them in order to feel that love, belonging, and acceptance. In a sense, speaking words of affirmation to others is a living eulogy.

This may surprise you, but "words of affirmation" are not one of my top love languages. They're not even close to the first. Whenever my husband and I led premarital or relationship counseling, we asked couples to take the love language test with us. We did that every time. We knew that over time things change and what we once valued might not be what we still valued. This is just a side note, but the same is true for the spiritual gifts test. If you haven't taken either a spiritual gifts test or the love language test recently, you should. Don't be surprised if the results aren't what they used to be.

Before my dad got sick, whenever I took the five love languages tests, "gifts" was off the chart. It literally stood head and shoulders above all the other love languages. John, my husband, always complained it was because I just liked "getting" stuff. That's not really the case, not if you fully understand what the love language of gifts entails. It is so much more than receiving something. It's about the thoughtful, purposeful, intentional care and forethought that goes into getting the gift. I do, however, have several family members whose love language is, you guessed it, "words of affirmation," so I have lots of practice.

In late 2018, our family received three gut punches back-to-back in a short period of time. First, my dad had surgery right before Thanksgiving due to a pituitary tumor pushing on his optic nerve. It seemed simple enough;

have surgery, remove the tumor, and life would go on. Sure, dad might not regain his full vision in that eye since the tumor had already caused it to blur, but we could deal with that and make any necessary adjustments. My dad did well at Thanksgiving, considering he had just been discharged from the hospital.

During that holiday, my dad called a family meeting to discuss his wishes, should anything happen to him. He hadn't had a living will, a DNR, or a medical power of attorney before the surgery and the medical staff recommended he discuss these items with his family. We sat around the table, filling out paperwork and discussing the details. Little did we know, my dad's health would change for the worse within a matter of days.

Shortly after Thanksgiving, my dad began to experience problems from many of the medical issues he was diagnosed with during his stay in the hospital after surgery. The most significant was his loss of muscle strength in his legs and inability to walk safely up the stairs. He had to use the handrail to pull himself up. When he reached the top and there was no longer something to hold onto, he became wobbly and was in danger of falling backwards. In fact, he had a hard time walking altogether and needed a cane and then a walker.

On Christmas Eve, we took two phone calls. One regarding my aunt, who was going into hospice care after years of being in remission after successfully fighting off lung cancer. The other was from a very close friend letting us know he had just been diagnosed with pancreatic cancer. The holidays that year were less than joyful.

2019 was a year of incredible highs and extreme lows as we ended up losing my dad, my aunt, and my friend. But there was even more loss our family sustained as you will read in the following timeline of events. Some people joke about surviving 2020 and the Covid pandemic. I say 2020 was a breeze compared to all we endured in 2019.

Here's a brief timeline of some of that year's extreme highs and lows.

- March: My aunt died
- April 1st: (worst April Fool's Day on record): our friend died
- April 7th: Our son got married, and our friend's

memorial service was held

- May: In a 4-day period, we celebrated my husband's 50th Birthday; we experienced betrayal and loss of relationship with people at our church; Our new daughter-in-law's mother committed suicide. Two days later, I was on a plane across the country for a ministry-speaking trip.
- September: My dad died

Since I had been teaching on the topic of speaking and pronouncing blessings for over fifteen years, I intentionally made a point to speak words of affirmation and impart living eulogies to my dad, my aunt, and our friend every chance I got before they passed.

I try to make it a habit to not just release "living eulogies" to only those who are sick or dying but to others in my sphere of influence as well. I want to be sure the people in my life know what they mean to me. I want to continually honor them while they are living just as much as I want to honor and memorialize them once they are gone. I know I am not alone in this. Personally though, I have lost many friends and family, had too many regrets over years of words left unspoken. Thankfully, I am confident my dad, my aunt, and our friend knew just how I felt and how much they meant to me.

I credit 2019 as the year my husband started to save money, because it was also the year my love language began to change from "gifts" to "quality time." I didn't shop as much to buy "gifts" for people. Oh, don't get me wrong. I'm still a gifts person. But now, I want to spend time and make memories with the ones I love. I think of spending time together as a gift I can give now. It's still a shock to me that "words of affirmation" hasn't taken over either of the top two spots, but it's a close third now.

What would it look like if we began giving living eulogies to those around us? How would it change us? How would it change those receiving our words? And how would it change our world?

I believe it would profoundly change not just our relationships, but also the atmosphere around us. There would be people filled with life and hopeful expectation of what tomorrow would bring. It matters when we declare other's value and importance. They are changed, we are changed, and our world is changed for the better. Let's be intentional in speaking blessings, words of affirmation, and honor to one another. After all, speaking living eulogies to others is exactly what we are commanded to do. Scripture gives a direct order to *"bless (encourage) one another everyday as long as it is still called today"* (Hebrews 3:13).

Legacy Builders

Prayer

Father, Your word says that You have given us the Holy Spirit to be our teacher and guide. Release the Spirit to teach and show me to see the good in others. Help me to be intentional about speaking words of honor and life towards others, not just today, but every day of my life. Reveal to me any place where I have been holding back my "living eulogies" for others and help me to begin releasing them to those in my life today. Amen.

Reflection

When was the last time you spoke a living eulogy to someone?

What is your love language? How about your spouse or a close friend?

Do you speak your love language when showing your love and care for others? Or theirs?

Blessing in Action

Choose a family member to speak a living eulogy to today.

Chapter 5
Are Blessings Biblical?

God blessed them and said to them ...
Genesis 1:28a NIV

In the early 2000's, I was part of a teaching team that held "Hearing God" classes at our church. We noticed people were hungry for more after the initial beginner classes were finished, so we began praying about what to offer as an option for more advanced prophetic training. When I first proposed teaching *Speaking and Pronouncing Blessings* to the advanced classes, one of my spiritual grandfathers, a mentor, and a church elder, Papa Carl, looked directly into my eyes with a challenge. Then he smiled slightly, almost smirking and asked, "Are blessings even Biblical?"

"Oh YES!" I emphatically replied. I was more than a tad frustrated he asked the question, but I also knew he was issuing a challenge. Well, if you know me, I didn't let this moment pass me by.

Challenge Accepted!

Of course, blessings are Biblical. I just needed to gather my evidence and present it to Papa Carl at our advanced prophetic training. I would go on to create a new curriculum for these classes, which I have now incorporated into my own Dare2Hear Part 2 *Hearing from God* classes.

All that to say, YES! Blessings are Biblical; in fact, God's first act after creating Adam and Eve was to speak a blessing.

> *God blessed them and said to them, "Be fruitful*
> *and increase in number; fill the earth and subdue*
> *it. Rule over the fish in the sea and the birds in the*
> *sky and over every living creature that moves on*
> *the ground."*
>
> Genesis 1:28 NIV

We see the first blessing referenced again just a few chapters later in Genesis when the fuller story of how God created mankind unfolded.

> *He created them male and female and blessed them*
> *and called them "Mankind" in the day they were*
> *created.*
>
> Genesis 5:2 NIV

Remember when I mentioned that if God says something once it's important, but if He repeats it a second time, we know He is serious about that topic? Yes, if there is a reiteration throughout the Scriptures, we had better pay attention because it's a crucial and essential part of our relationship and walk with Him.

With my "theory of repetition" in play, we can see God blesses Adam and Eve, and then it is mentioned again in the detailed retelling of how He created Adam and Eve. However, God didn't stop pronouncing blessings after He created the earth. He continued with a pattern of blessing His creation. The act of blessing is so important to the heart of God that not only does He bless His people, but we see the people of God incorporating blessings into their lives as well. We find examples of His blessings in both the Old and New Testaments. Here are just a few more examples for you throughout Scripture.

First, let's look at how God blessed His people. After the flood, when Noah and his family disembarked from the ark and were about to begin living on land again, they immediately built an altar to God (Genesis 8:17-22). It was during this interaction God gave Noah, his family, and all the animals the same command and blessing He gave Adam and Eve.

> *Bring out every kind of living creature that is with*
> *you—the birds, the animals, and all the creatures*

> *that move along the ground—so they can multiply*
> *on the earth and be fruitful and increase in number*
> *on it.*
> Genesis 8:17 NIV

God is in the business of repeating specific messages. I believe this shows the importance and priority God placed on these topics and issues. First, we see God conversing and giving Noah and his family instructions about what He wants them to do. Then, upon the pleasant-smelling aroma of Noah's sacrifice to God, He continues to instruct them by BLESSING them. Yes, that's right, He gives the official command, instructing them to be fruitful and multiply, and He turns it into a blessing.

> *Then God blessed Noah and his sons, saying to*
> *them, "Be fruitful and increase in number and fill*
> *the earth ..."*
> Genesis 9:1 NIV

However, God doesn't stop there. He adds more blessing and instruction for Noah and his family (see Genesis 9:1-17). He circles back again in verse 7, and for a third time, He instructs them by saying "be fruitful and increase in number..."

> *As for you, be fruitful and increase in number;*
> *multiply on the earth and increase upon it.*
> Genesis 9:7 NIV

I would say God wants this instructive message, turned blessing, to be prominent in their minds from that day forward. He did not want them to forget its importance. God then strengthens and solidifies the blessing and commission He is bestowing upon Noah and his family by making a covenant with them, further strengthening the blessing.

> *Then God said to Noah and his sons with him: "I*
> *now establish my covenant with you and with your*
> *descendants after you ..."*
> Genesis 9:8-9 NIV

Covenants are binding agreements. A covenant, as defined by the Scriptures, is a solemn and binding relationship that is meant to last a lifetime.[32]

Blessings, Promises, and Covenants

Blessings, Promises, and Covenants, oh my ... what are they and is there a difference?

It's easy to get confused sometimes if we don't understand the differences in terminology used in Scripture and Christendom. Sometimes words get interchanged, but they don't always mean the same thing. For example, in the Psalms, soul and spirit are often confused as the same thing when in fact, they are not. The spirit is the part of us created to commune with God, while the soul is our mind, will, and emotions. You would have to go back to the original Greek and Hebrew language in some cases to figure out which word the author really intended.

I previously shared both the definition of blessings and covenant. But what is a promise, and how do they all relate to one another? Let's recap, so there's no confusion.

> **Blessing**: A blessing is the act of declaring favor and goodness upon others. A blessing was also one way of asking for God's divine favor to rest upon others.[33]

> **Promise**: a declaration or assurance that something will or will not be done, given, etc., by one:[34] To make a declaration to another, which binds the promiser in honor, conscience, or law, to do or forbear some act; To assure one by a promise or binding declaration.[35]

> **Covenant**: Covenants are binding agreements that are meant to last a lifetime.[36]

As nouns, the difference between **blessing** and **promise** is that blessing is some kind of divine or supernatural aid or reward while **promise** is an oath or affirmation. a vow.

> As a verb, **promise** means:
> To commit to something or action; to make an oath; make a vow.[37]

> As nouns the difference between **promise** and **covenant** is that **promise** is an oath or affirmation or a vow, while a **covenant** is a legal agreement to do or not do a particular thing.
>
> As verbs the difference between **promise** and **covenant** is that to **promise** is to commit to some thing or action; or make an oath; make a vow, while to **covenant** is to enter into, or **promise** something by a **covenant**.[38]

As you can see, there are similarities in the definitions and ever-so-slight differences, too. I look at one as building and adding a layer to the next. A blessing is a request or act of declaring God's goodness and favor. A promise adds another layer to the blessing, becoming a declaration of honor or an assurance. Then finally, a covenant adds another layer to a promise which is a legally binding agreement. We also know from Scripture that God does not lie (see Numbers 23:19; Titus 1:2; Hebrews 6:18), so if he blesses, makes a promise, or commits to a covenant, He will be faithful to see it fulfilled.

Let's take a deeper dive to understand the concept of covenants better. There are two kinds: bilateral and unilateral agreements. In most cases, we think of covenants, like a marriage covenant, as being between two equal parties, which means that it's a bilateral agreement. The bond is sealed by both parties vowing, often by oath, that each having equal privileges and responsibilities, will carry out their assigned roles.[39] However, we also have covenants established and initiated by God. God determined the elements and confirmed His covenant with humanity. This means the covenant is unilateral. Humans are recipients, not contributors; they are not expected to offer elements to the bond. Instead, they are called to accept the covenant as offered, to keep it as demanded, and to receive the results that God, by oath, assures us will not be withheld.[40]

The entire chapter of Genesis 15 is a perfect example of God establishing a covenant with man. I encourage you to take time to read it and pay close attention to the dialogue between God and Abram. In verses 13-16, God even speaks a prophetic, future-driven blessing about Abram's descendants and then proceeds to put him into a deep sleep and make a covenant with him.

On that day the LORD *made a covenant with Abram ...*
Genesis 15:18 NIV

Are Blessings Biblical?

Of course, the best way to prove if something is Biblical truth is to look at the Bible. If there's one thing my conservative church roots have taught me, it's the importance of Scripture. And after years of pastoring and teaching, I know just what questions most skeptics will ask when it comes to something being Biblical. They are: Are there more than one or two examples of blessings in the Bible? Are blessings just in the Old Testament or do they occur in the New Testament as well?

You already know where I stand on the first question. If God says it once, it's enough for me. But when He repeats something, it's a very important message. The next question addressing both the Old and New Testament boggles my mind as well. But trust me ... it matters to some. Why? Some believe if it's only in the Old Testament, then it isn't as relevant. For the record, I wholeheartedly disagree with that sentiment. Yet, I still hear this argument. Once, I had someone tell me we didn't need to read or study the Old Testament anymore because we needed to be living by the New Testament. I also had a pastor inform me that if it wasn't in both the Old and New, but mostly the New, then it wasn't for today. Uhmmm, that's not exactly true. I often quote Hebrews 13:8.

> *Jesus Christ is the same yesterday, today, and forever. (NLT)*

If He did it then, He is doing it today and will continue to do it forever! Every concept, story, idea, and thought in the New Testament is tied to the Old Testament. Go ahead, I challenge you to take a concept or idea in the New Testament and start to pull the strings to uncover where it originates. It will lead you to the Old Testament! But much more than that. The Old Testament is not just a bunch of good ole stories about ancient people. They are testimonies of God's goodness and His love. The Old Testament reveals to us God's very nature, character, and values. We can't have a complete picture of who God is without both Testaments.

I digress. Let me get off my soapbox for a minute and assure you that YES, blessings are Biblical. You will find them through the entirety of

Scripture. I have already shared several examples in previous chapters, but here are some more.

God blessed Adam and Eve, and therefore all humanity when he told them to be fruitful and multiply. Here are some more examples in the Old Testament of God blessing individuals:

- God blessed Noah and his sons in Genesis 9:1-7
- God blessed Abraham in Genesis12:1-3
- Jacob wrestled with God and won't let go until God blessed him in Genesis 32:24-32
- God blesses all of Israel in Numbers 6:22-27
- King David asks God to bless him and his household in II Samuel 7:29

And here are even more examples in the Old Testament of individuals blessing others:

- Isaac blessed Jacob in Genesis 27:30-38
- This blessing was intended for Esau, but Jacob stole it. In this blessing, we see Isaac bestow a blessing upon Jacob.
- Jacob blesses Ephraim and Manasseh in Genesis 48
- Aaron's Blessing for Israel in Numbers 6:22-27
- Boaz is greeted by a blessing in Ruth 2:4

In the New Testament, we find several examples of blessings revolving around and involving Jesus himself:

- A prophetic blessing was given just after Jesus was born:

    Then Simeon blessed them and said to Mary His mother, "Behold, this Child is destined for the fall and rising of many in Israel, and for a sign which will be spoken against, so that the thoughts of many hearts will be revealed. And a sword will pierce your own soul too."
    Luke 2:34-35 NKJV

- Jesus began his Ministry with an announcement of a blessing from God:

   This is my Son, whom I love, with him I am well pleased.
   Matthew 3:17 NIV

- Jesus speaks several blessings during His sermon on the mount and the Beatitudes

   "Blessed are the poor in spirit, For theirs is the kingdom of heaven. Blessed are those who mourn, For they shall be comforted. Blessed are the meek, For they shall inherit the earth. Blessed are those who hunger and thirst for righteousness, For they shall be filled. Blessed are the merciful, For they shall obtain mercy. Blessed are the pure in heart, For they shall see God. Blessed are the peacemakers, For they shall be called sons of God. Blessed are those who are persecuted for righteousness' sake, For theirs is the kingdom of heaven. "Blessed are you when they revile and persecute you, and say all kinds of evil against you falsely for My sake."
   Matt 5: 3-11 NIV

- Jesus Blessed Children
   "And He took the children His arms, placed His hands on them and blessed them."
   Mark 10:16 NIV

- Jesus' last act before He left earth was to impart a blessing

   ... "he lifted up his hands and blessed them. While he was blessing them he left them and was taken into heaven."
   Luke 24:50-51 NIV

- We are to Continue blessing

> *Finally, all of you should be of one mind, full of sympathy toward each other, loving one another with tender hearts and humble minds. Don't repay evil for evil. Don't retaliate when people say unkind things about you. Instead, pay them back with a blessing. That is what God wants you to do, and he will bless you for it. For the Scriptures say, "If you want a happy life and good days, keep your tongue from speaking evil, and keep your lips from telling lies."*
>
> I Peter 3:8-9 NLT

Probably the most Popular Biblical Blessing in the Bible can be found in Numbers 6:22-27. There is so much richness to these five verses alone that I have dedicated the entire next chapter to breaking it down. I pray that I made the case to satisfy even the greatest skeptic that not only are blessings Biblical, but they are also, or rather should be, an essential element in the life of a believer.

Legacy Builders

Prayer

God, thank You for the Bible, the living and true Word of God. Thank You for making it a solid foundation I can stand upon and a compass I can direct my life with. Thank You for remaining the same throughout the ages. God, Your word says You do not lie, but forgive me for the times I didn't believe You or Your Word. I want to receive and walk in the fullness of all the blessings, promises, and covenants in Your Word and those spoken over my life. Help me to do so. In Jesus' Name, Amen.

Reflection

Has anyone ever spoken a blessing over your life? Who was it, and what did they say?

Is there a blessing, promise, or a covenant in God's word that you have a hard time believing is for you? If so, which one and why?

Blessing in Action

Find a blessing, promise, or covenant in the Bible and begin to proclaim it over your life today.

Chapter 6
Aaron's Blessing

Tell Aaron and his sons, "This is how you are to bless the Israelites ..."

Numbers 6:23 NIV

The Aaronic blessing found in Numbers 6 is a clear example of what a blessing is and what blessings can accomplish in our lives.

The Eternal One bless and keep you.
May He make His face shine upon you and be gracious to you.
The Eternal lift up His countenance to look upon you and give you peace.

Numbers 6:24-26 The Voice

God insisted that Moses tell Aaron and his sons to speak and pronounce this blessing over the children of Israel. This blessing is still spoken today and not just to Jewish sons and daughters on the evening of Shabbat in homes. It is spoken regularly in Synagogues and churches worldwide, as a blessing and a benediction. But why? Because it is hope-filled, powerful, prophetic, encouraging, and shows God's love and care for His people.

The Priestly Blessing of Aaron, or the Aaronic Blessing as the Jewish people refer to it, was given to the people of Israel as they prepared to leave Mt Sinai. Bible commentaries believe they had been camping there for at least a year to a year-and-a-half and were about to continue their journey through the wilderness to the promised land. This journey would lead them to the land promised to Abraham and Sarah, and when they took possession, would be a covenant promise fulfilled. The blessing in Numbers 6 is located in the middle of many instructions from Numbers 1 through Numbers 10 which God gave to Moses in preparation for their departure.

It's important to remember that during their time camping at Mt. Sinai, the children of Israel were constantly grumbling and complaining about one thing or another. They also betrayed God when they made a golden calf to worship. As if that wasn't bad enough, they rejected God in Exodus 19 when they chose not to be consecrated and set apart as holy so they could meet with God. God wanted to reestablish a relationship with his chosen people but because they were afraid, it didn't happen. Yet God still loved them, and to reinforce that love, He wanted to bless and remind them of who He is.

We already know the Old Testament word for blessing is *barak* which literally means to kneel before someone or give something of value to another. Can you pull up a mental picture of what is happening here? After all the heartache, whining, complaining, rejection, and betrayal, God still chose to, in essence, *kneel* before the Children of Israel and bestow a blessing upon them. This blessing is something God deems of great value. He blesses them through Aaron and his sons as he continually spoke the words over them as a reminder of who He was, what He is doing, and why He traveled with them.

Numbers 6 is the model for how we are to bless. It's packed full of God's blessings, as well as His promises to us.

The Priestly Blessing

The Lord said to Moses, "Tell Aaron and his sons,
'This is how you are to bless the Israelites. Say to
them:
"'"The Lord bless you
and keep you;
the Lord make his face shine on you
and be gracious to you;
the Lord turn his face toward you
and give you peace."'

66

*"So they will put my name on the Israelites, and I
will bless them."*
Numbers 6:22-27 NIV

We can learn seven things from this passage about what a blessing is
supposed to do. The entire passage is five verses, but the blessing only
comprises the last three. I like to look at several translations to get a
fuller picture of the message the words convey, so here are a few more
translations to look at as we dive deeper into this.

*Then the LORD said to Moses, "Instruct Aaron
and his sons to bless the people of Israel with this
special blessing: 'May the LORD bless you and
protect you. May the LORD smile on you and be
gracious to you. May the LORD show you his favor
and give you, his peace.' This is how Aaron and his
sons will designate the Israelites as my people, and
I myself will bless them."*
Numbers 6:22-27 NLT

*And the Lord spoke to Moses, saying: "Speak to
Aaron and his sons, saying, 'This is the way you
shall bless the children of Israel. Say to them: "The
Lord bless you and keep you; The Lord make His
face shine upon you, And be gracious to you; The
Lord lift up His countenance upon you, And give
you peace."' "So they shall put My name on the
children of Israel, and I will bless them."*
Numbers 6:22-27 NKJV

*(Continuing instruction to Moses) Tell Aaron and
his sons to bless the Israelites by saying, The
Eternal One bless and keep you. May He make His
face shine upon you and be gracious to you. The
Eternal lift up His countenance to look upon you
and give you peace. In this way, they will set My
name upon the Israelites, and I will bless them.*
Numbers 6:22-27 The Voice

Numbers 6 is a powerful passage conveying hope that God would do the following seven things:

1. Give favor and protection –

    The Lord bless you and keep you;
    Numbers 6:24 NKJV

    'May the LORD bless you and protect you
    Numbers 6:24 NLT

Verse 24 conveys that not only will God bless his people, but he will protect and keep them. God, the Good Shepherd, will guard and keep watch over His children. Just as a shepherd protects his flock, God will watch over them. They will not only have the protection of God but His favor as well.

2. Be pleased

    May the LORD smile on you.
    Numbers 6:25 NLT

    May He make His face shine upon you.
    Numbers 6:25 The Voice

Verse 25 demonstrates God is pleased and smiling down on us. This is a beautiful picture showing God is pleased with His people when His face shines upon us. Just like a proud Father looking upon His child beaming brightly with a smile from ear to ear, God is pleased and delighted with us. This portion is also about being welcomed in His presence. I will share more about the presence in verse 26 below.

3. Be merciful and compassionate

    and be gracious to you.
    Numbers 6:25 NIV

Verse 25 communicates God will graciously extend us His mercy and compassion. I find it interesting that out of all the translations I listed above, all use the exact same wording when we come to this part of the blessing. When looking at the definition from Strong's Concordance[41], we see the entire phrase conveys the meaning, not just the word *gracious*. To be gracious means to bend or stoop in kindness and bestow mercy, have pity on, and grant favor to someone.

4. Give His approval –

> *the LORD turn his face toward you.*
> > Numbers 6:26 NIV

> *The Eternal lift up His countenance to look upon*
> > Numbers 6:26 The Voice

Verse 26 establishes God will give us His approval by turning toward us. In Psalms 27:9, we see God turns His face away from those He disapproves of. But here, God says He will turn toward His people and lift His countenance toward us. Psalms 4:6 further solidifies this picture of delight and approval when God's face lights up as He looks upon us. This is also an invitation to come into His presence. Much like King Ahasuerus (Xerxes I) extended his scepter to Queen Esther as a sign of his approval, granting her access to his throne room, God is saying He is offering His approval to us as His children. He wants to be with us, to look upon us, and for us to be in His presence. Under the New Testament Covenant, it means even more because of Christ's sacrifice at the cross. Not only did His death pay the price for our sins, but upon His death, the veil in the temple was torn in half from top to bottom granting us full access. This one act by Jesus removed the veil separating us from God, granting us access to His throne room!

5. Give Peace

> ... *give you peace.*
>
> Numbers 6:26 NIV

Verse 26 is another example where all the translations listed above use the exact same wording when we get to this part: That God would give you His peace. Peace is the Shâlôm of God. The word shalom is more than just simple peace. It conveys the idea of contentment, completeness, wholeness, well-being, and harmony.[42]

> Shâlôm[43] means completeness, soundness, welfare, peace
>
> A. completeness (in number)
> B. safety, soundness (in body)
> C. welfare, health, prosperity
> D. peace, quiet, tranquility, contentment
> E. peace, friendship
>   a. of human relationships
>   i. with God especially in covenant relationship
> F. peace (from war)

The word *shalom* beautifully encapsulates powerful blessings on multiple levels!

As you look at the definition of Shâlôm, you'll see the Shâlôm peace of God can also mean "the absence of war." But how can this make sense if God is preparing the Israelites to possess the Promised Land and destroy cities?

Brenda Fawkes, a blogger, in her online article, *Shalom, the Peace that Passes Understanding* discusses this very aspect of God preparing the Israelites for war, yet imparting peace to them.

The Aaronic Blessing refers to an inner peace and completeness brought on by sharing in His countenance and protection. That was the blessing that Israel needed! Israel rarely experienced times of outward peace, but even in the midst of battle, they had an inward rest brought on by the presence of the Lord, regardless of the outward circumstances. So should it be for us as well.[44]

6. God's Name

> they will **set My name upon** the Israelites ...
> Numbers 6:27a The Voice

> will designate the Israelites as my people ...
> Numbers 6:27a NLT

Verse 27a is powerful and establishes God's intention to put His name on them, marking them as His own. The verse as explained in Strong's Concordance[45] indicates more than just God's name being placed on the people. God's name includes His reputation, His fame, and His Glory. This also implies honor and authority. God's name is renowned throughout the land. When the Israelites are about to take Jericho, spying out the land, we see a report of God's fame. Rahab spoke to the spies and said to them:

> I know that the LORD has given you this land and that a great fear of you has fallen on us, so that all who live in this country are melting in fear because of you. We have heard how the LORD dried up the water of the Red Sea for you when you came out of Egypt, and what you did to Sihon and Og, the two kings of the Amorites east of the Jordan, whom

you completely destroyed. When we heard of it, our hearts melted in fear and everyone's courage failed because of you, for the LORD your God is God in heaven above and on the earth below.

Joshua 2:9-11 NIV

Putting God's name on the people emphasizes His reputation and acknowledges He is the divine source of all blessing. The people now *wear* God's name and bear His reputation. The same is true for us and others when we bless them in the name of God. His name should be worn in a way so all will know, see, and believe in Him.

7. God Blesses

... I myself will bless them.

Numbers 6:27b NLT

... and I will bless them.

Numbers 6:27b NKJV

Verse 27b is the final line of this short but power-packed blessing. We see God Himself is going to bless the children of Israel. Yes, Aaron and his sons are the ones who speak it forth, but God has every intention of being the one to bestow this valuable blessing and see it come to fruition. The word for blessing is again the word *barak* which means to kneel. Another implication of this word is an act of adoration. God is exhibiting His love for His people by personally blessing them.

When we ask God to bless others by intentionally speaking and pronouncing blessings, we ask Him to do these seven things above as well. God is the one who brings about the blessing. The blessing we speak will not only help the one receiving it, but it will also demonstrate these three things:

1. God's Love
2. Our love for others
3. Provide a model of caring for others

In an online article, cartoonist, teacher, and Pastor Steve Thomason says: "This blessing is not just a pretty poem. It is not just a nice thing to say at the end of a worship service. **It is the very heart of the Gospel.** God created and continually brings all things into being out of love and for the purpose of loving interdependence, relationship, and true peace. That is what the Garden of Eden represented. It is God's ultimate vision for creation, no matter how long it takes to get there."[46]

I've had the opportunity to speak to some Jewish Christian Pastors and ask a few questions. One of them, Pastor Gary Fishman, spoke with me at length regarding a Rabbi's interpretation and explanation for each portion of the Aaronic blessing. Pastor Gary confirmed much of what I already understood but went on to add some depth and a few revelations.

From a Rabbi's perspective, Numbers 6 is a picture of a Father who kneels down to give a gift and also joyfully lifts a child above his head, fully delighting in the child. A Rabbi teaches that God meets us right where we are, which is powerful for those who feel unworthy. Additionally, God surrounds us and keeps a hedge of protection around us, like a Shepherd creates a barrier of safety for his sheep. We need to remember that God's face lights up when He sees us, and He is proud of His people. One powerful revelation Pastor Gary mentioned is this; as a Christian believer another dimension is added when you read Numbers 6 in connection with Philippians 2:7. In the context of the word *barak,* meaning to kneel down and give a gift, this Scripture tells us Jesus not only lowered Himself, but He was also born in a lowly place.

> *... but emptied himself, by taking the form of a*
> *servant, being born in the likeness of men.*
> Philippians 2:7 ESV

Jesus indeed did empty himself for us by coming to earth. God knelt and gave us the gift of His Son, Jesus. This was God's answer and blessing for humanity.

Legacy Builders

Prayer

God, thank you for giving us the gift of Your son, Jesus.

Jesus, thank you for emptying Yourself for me. Thank You for Your sacrifice of dying on the cross so that I, too, am accepted and grafted in as a child of God. Because of this, I can receive the fullness of the blessing God released over the children of Israel. I declare it over my life today.

Lord bless and keep me; Lord shine Your face upon me, And be gracious to me; Lord lift Your countenance upon me, And give me peace. Lord, put Your name on me, and bless me.

God, You are the Good Shepherd. You place a hedge of protection around me and keep me safe. You delight in me and extend your favor toward me. Release Your Shalom Peace over my life and every situation I face. Amen.

Reflection

When you think about the definition of the word *barak*, what mental picture comes to mind?

Which of the seven points from the Blessing of Aaron spoke to you the most and why?

Consider the Shalom Peace of God. Is it evident in your life today? If so, how? If not, what can you do to change that?

Blessing in Action

Continue to daily declare out loud over yourself Aaron's blessing from Numbers 6. Also, ask God who else outside your family you need to speak it over.

Chapter 7
Are Blessings for Today?

But encourage one another daily, as long as it is called "Today."

Hebrews 3:13 NIV

My spiritual mentor, Papa Carl, was always a challenger but in a good way. After I brought back the in-depth, well-researched answer to his question in Chapter 5, "Are blessings even Biblical?" His reply was another challenge with a side of sarcasm. "Ok, so they are Biblical, but are they for today?"

Papa Carl brought out the best in me and was forever asking questions to motivate me to dig deeper. He went home to be with the Lord several years ago but his legacy lives on in the many other people we taught together throughout the years as well as in my own life.

Again, the answer is YES, most definitely, blessings are for today. However, in my opinion, the concept of speaking and pronouncing a blessing is a lost art. It's not something most people do anymore nor is it commonly taught in our churches. Yes, we read about it in Scripture, and we see that it was an important enough concept to God that He gave a blessing to Moses to speak over the people. Even before the famous blessing of Numbers 6, we read about God blessing Abraham, Abraham blessing Isaac, Isaac blessings Jacob, Jacob blessing his grandsons ... and on and on. The power and importance of the blessing have been lost over the generations and I think it's time we revisit their importance and reinstate them as a part of our life.

We are called to be light in a dark world (see Matthew 5:16) and we are commanded to bring positive encouragement to a negative and dying world (see Hebrews 13:3).

There is power in our words alone.

> *Death and Life are in the power of the tongue ...*
> Proverbs 18:21 ESV

By speaking simple words, we can bring life or death. Everyone needs to hear positive words of encouragement and hope, no matter how hard-hearted or calloused a person may seem. It's important to note if positive encouragement is not given, the negative will automatically be assumed.

For example, growing up, my parents always referred to my sister as the pretty one and I was referenced as the smart one. I'm not sure what my sister ever thought about those labels but for me, they formed a core belief in myself. Because positive encouragement affirming I was pretty was never given, only that I was smart, the negative was assumed—I wasn't pretty. Remember the story of Marcus from Kerry Kirkwood's book who became a painter? His father hadn't given him the positive encouragement a child needs. The only time he heard something positive, that he was good at painting, he held on to it and assumed all the other things he did or accomplished never mattered. If positive encouragement isn't given, human nature automatically assumes the worst.

Another example occurred recently. One night, after a particularly long week of ministry sessions and healing appointments, I sat outside while my husband was working on a project. He asked a simple question; "Do you ever get feedback from the people you minister to or walk-through healing with who say your ministry has changed them?" I immediately got irritated and defensive. At the time, I bit my tongue and responded, "Yes, in fact I've received a beautiful message today thanking me for the session the night before." Later, I even pulled up the note and read it word for word to reinforce my work's importance and value.

I knew my inward reaction to his simple question was off. I just didn't know what button it was pushing. Thankfully, I held back from reacting and emotionally spewing words I couldn't take back later. I was tired from a long week. Ministry and healing work are wonderful and exciting, especially when you see people set free from bondages and struggles which have plagued them for a long time. However, it can also be draining for the minister. It's physically and emotionally taxing, but God sustains.

I have a t-shirt that says, "If my mouth doesn't say it, my face will." That pretty much sums me up. Truth be told, I can't hide my emotions and feelings very well. I may not say how I feel about something, but you can usually read it all over my face. Thank goodness my husband was preoccupied with his power tools and wasn't watching my face. However, while I may have held my tongue from lashing out and saying mean things, the tenor of my words spoke volumes regarding my irritation at his question.

After his initial question and my response, I got up and went inside. I could feel the agitation in my soul, I was overly bothered. It took me a while to process what was going on. His question seemed innocent and anyone hearing it would have said so. However, past conversations and arguments about how hard I work or the long hours I put in with little to show came to my mind. I was already physically tired, which also didn't help keep my emotions in check, and I went from zero to sixty with my annoyance and frustrated feelings. What I heard in his question was, "Does what you do even matter?"

Later, when I shared with him what I was feeling, he nodded and replied, "I wondered what was going on. I could hear the irritation and defensive tone in your response. I was simply trying to connect with you and talk about your week. I wasn't questioning your value or worth."

Why did I automatically assume the negative in his question? Because the positive wasn't spoken. There was no encouragement or acknowledgment that I worked hard and offered a service that helped people. There were no atta-girls for a job well done, only questions.

The lesson here is simple, don't assume someone will automatically know what you're feeling, thinking, or implying. They only have your words to go on. We've all heard stories from others about how they wondered if their parents, or someone else significant in their life, really loved them. We might wonder how this can be. It's simple, the individual just

79

assumed the person knew they loved them by their actions and deeds, not because they spoke the words. Make sure to speak up and speak often. Give positive encouragement, speak words of affirmation, and reinforce the good every chance you get.

In previous chapters, we looked at both Old and New Testament Scriptures showing God blessing others. We have discussed how blessings are Biblical and how God repeats the message of blessings throughout the Bible as well. In Chapter 5 there are Biblical examples of how individuals can also bless others. In the New Testament, there are several other verses that come to mind; besides the ones I have already talked about which reinforce blessings are for today. While these Scriptures are not a direct command to bless, they do show us the basis for why we can bless others. They are:

> *Blessed be the God and Father of our Lord Jesus Christ, who has blessed us in Christ with every spiritual blessing in the heavenly places.*
> Ephesians 1:3 ESV

Because Christ has blessed us with every spiritual blessing, we can therefore allow those blessings to overflow to others. This allows us to not just be a blessing, but we can give blessings to others from our position in Christ. In case you don't know what it means to be positioned in Christ and to speak blessings from that place, I want to give a brief explanation. Please know, whole books have been written on the subject. Our position in Christ is that we are seated in heavenly places (see Ephesians 2:4-9; Romans 6:4), we are the righteousness of God (see Romans 3:22; Romans 6:18-19; 2 Corinthians 5:21; Philippians 3:9), and we are made Holy in Christ Jesus (see Hebrews 10:10-14). Our position has to do with our legal status, not necessarily our condition right now. By faith, we are justified in Christ (see Romans 3:24; Romans 5:1; Galatians 3:24), this position in Him is forever secure because we chose to believe by faith the work Christ did on the cross. Therefore, our position makes it possible for us to bless others. Understanding our identity and position in Christ is essential for walking in maturity. In the Bible, Paul uses his letter to the Ephesians to walk us step-by-step into who we are in Christ and how to be a Christ follower and a mature believer.

So let us come boldly to the throne of our gracious
God. There we will receive his mercy, and we will
find grace to help us when we need it most.

Hebrews 4:16 NLT

Matthew 10:8b tells us to freely give just as we have received. So, we can boldly approach God and ask Him to show us how to extend words of mercy and grace to others in need in the form of blessing.

Be devoted to tenderly loving your fellow believers
as members of one family. Try to outdo yourselves
in respect and honor of one another.

Romans 12:10 TPT

Blessing others is just one way we can show honor and respect. Yes, there are many other ways one can show honor but when we also pair Romans 12:10 with others like Hebrews 13:3 where we are commanded to encourage one another daily as long as it's today. Plus, in Romans 12:14 we are told to bless and not curse those who persecute us, which we will talk more in-depth about in the following chapter.

Blessings are most certainly for today and every day! In fact, in the New Testament, we see this same practice continuing from the Old Testament. Jesus began His earthly ministry with a blessing from His Father (see Matthew 3:17). He then models the act of blessing others through blessing children (see Mark 10:16). Jesus also releases blessings during His sermon on the mount (see Matthew 5: 3-11) and finally, His last act before leaving earth was to bless (see Luke 24:50-51)! Since Jesus Christ is the same yesterday, today, and forever (Hebrews 13:8), and we are to follow His example, then we should be imparting blessings too.

But encourage one another daily, as long as it
is called "Today," so that none of you may be
hardened by sin's deceitfulness.

Hebrews 13:3 NIV

81

Legacy Builders

Prayer

Father God, I recognize and acknowledge that blessings are important and powerful. I am sorry for not fully understanding their importance and allowing them to be an afterthought. I want to be light and life in a dark and dying world. Help me to reinstate blessings as an integral part of my daily life. Show me how I can speak encouragement to others. Amen.

Reflection

Can you recall a time when someone said something, and you automatically assumed the negative? What was it and why did you assume the worst?

Can you remember when someone spoke a good word to you that impacted your life?

Do the people around you know you love them because you have spoken it, or do you assume they just know?

Blessing in Action

Use words to intentionally tell your family and friends how much you love them.

Chapter 8
Blessings and Curses

Out of the same mouth proceed blessing and cursing ...

James 3:10 NKJV

In March of 2012, I received an invitation to join a group of intercessors and to teach about the importance and power of declaring the promises and blessings of God—with emphasis on going beyond petitioning heaven through prayer. The group's leader felt there was more they could do than just make requests through their prayers. She had heard my blessing teaching and felt this was an answer to how they could petition heaven more biblically. I shared my teaching on speaking and pronouncing blessings but I added a portion to it so I could specifically speak to intercessors. I had recently finished reading Kerry Kirkwood's book on *The Power of the Blessing* and I shared a few things from it that challenged me. The thoughts I shared were a challenge, not because I didn't believe what he wrote, they challenged me because I knew they were true. I am a person with a strong sense of justice. My alarm bells go off and things get wonky in my emotions when unjust things occur and go unpunished.

In Kerry's book, he shares a story about a pastor who cursed a strip club near his neighborhood daily.[47] The pastor was perplexed as to why the business didn't 'dry up and die' as he spoke. One day, as he was on his daily drive to curse the nightclub, the Lord spoke to him and asked, "Why are you cursing people I have given my life for—the same life I gave for you?" This question gave the pastor revelation that the issue wasn't the business itself but the blindness of those who patronized the business.[48] He decided to bless the people, instead of cursing the business. His blessing was simple yet powerful. He declared a blessing proclaiming that all of God's *"full intentions for their lives, from the moment they were formed, would come to fruition."*

It may be a challenging idea to wrap our minds around, especially when we see the damage particular businesses and individuals cause to others, but God does require us to bless and not curse. Blessing others does not mean we agree with the sin or *evil* we see occurring or that they participate in. Instead, we must recognize it's the goodness of God that brings people to repentance.

Within two weeks of the pastor's blessing, the owner of the strip club closed its doors without notice. " 'Cursing causes darkness to thrive and blessing turns things for righteousness' sake. The pastor learned a lesson many Christians never seem to grasp. Blessing is an attribute of God. This took a weight off the pastor's shoulders—the burden of having to punish his foes. A new strategy for spiritual warfare was opened to him."[49]

God protects and defends ALL His kids, even those who are not yet believers and those who have chosen to reject him blatantly. That was the new idea that rubbed up against my justice button and caused me discomfort. But again, I knew what Kerry had written was true.

As a mom, I can discipline my kids and talk about how they drive me crazy, but "don't you dare talk about them and try to discipline them yourself!" God is the same way, it's His job, not ours to bring correction and judgment upon others. Ours is to speak life over them and pray for God's intervention and for His plans to prevail in their lives.

The teaching setting was both in-person and via teleconference. A few attendees had questions, thanks, and appreciation for what I shared. Just when I thought I was finished, a woman's voice came through the phone. She said she appreciated my teaching but couldn't agree with blessing our state's current Governor. If I was a believer, then I must know the Governor was not a God-fearing believer and had made some horrible decisions in direct opposition to our Christian values and beliefs. She reiterated that she couldn't possibly bless the Governor and God wouldn't want her to, considering the *evil* she saw. It seemed like an eternity before she was done speaking and I was ready to respond.

Agent of Blessing

There was silence on the phone line. Not only that, but the silence in the room I was sitting in was deafening as well. All eyes were on me, no one said anything, and they just waited for me to respond. I think a few were even holding their breath. When the woman on the phone first began speaking, and I realized she was directing her comments to me, openly attacking what I taught, I began praying in my spiritual language. I did my best to keep my face from showing my emotions, but I am not sure if I fully succeeded. There were less than twenty people in the room, the rest were dialing in from the safety and comfort of their sofas.

All right, Holy Spirit now is the time to reveal the truth to me, I thought. I needed to respond, I just couldn't sit idly by and allow her to diminish the teaching or the Biblical truths the Lord had given me to share. I continued to pray in tongues while my brain ran rampant. *This was God's message, I was just the delivery person*, I coached myself. *There had to be some Biblical story to rebut her objections.*

The Holy Spirit indeed came through and prompted me to recall the story of Saul to Paul. I explained to the group that God had a plan and purpose for Saul. He didn't want Saul killed, thrown in jail, or destroyed. Saul had a destiny to fulfill but not as Saul. God needed room to move upon Saul, change his heart and mind about who He was, and release him with his new name, Paul, into his newfound destiny. Saul was zealous and passionate about killing Christians. He truly believed he was doing the right thing until Jesus met him on the road to Damascus. That one encounter with Jesus changed everything. Saul became Paul and the zeal and passion he had to kill the disciples of Christ turned around. He began working with the disciples and sharing the truth of the Gospel of Christ with all who would listen. If God could change Saul's heart, He would surely change our Governor's heart.

I went on to share that by blessing the Governor, we were not agreeing to bless his actions. Instead, we were blessing the Governor to come into agreement and perfect alignment with the plans and purposes of God. God has a destiny for each person. He has from before the foundation of the world (Ephesians 1:4). The choice is theirs and ours whether we will choose God or choose our own path, which ultimately leads us to destruction (Proverbs 14:12).

I could tell by the reactions on the faces of the individuals in the room they had understood. I'm not sure what those on the phone thought but there was a long silence until the leader picked up and began leading the prayer time. And I silently prayed what I shared would be taken to heart and implemented somehow. I wasn't entirely sure what would transpire after I left.

> *Bless those who persecute you; bless and do not curse.*
>
> Romans 12:14 NIV

Later that week, I received the following portion of an email from the lady who invited me to speak.

> Dear Debbie:
>
> Thank you so much for sharing what God gave you for us, as it was edifying, encouraging, and uplifting—just what we needed to "Dare 2 Hear" as intercessors. Reaching higher and declaring His Word, not just petitioning. We have begun to go in that direction, so your word gave the additional impetus to be bolder. It was a blessing to see you again and to be reminded of your excellent service to the body of Christ—spilling over with joy and enthusiasm.
>
> You are always welcome to join us, should the Lord prompt you.

All I could think was, *Praise God! They got it.* They understood our words are important, and it matters what we speak and pray. They understood we are to be agents of blessing. Truthfully, I understood firsthand what the women on the phone struggled with. God had worked on my heart for some time about intentionally being an agent of blessing toward those I perceived as my enemies, as well as those whom I perceived, were doing wrong and heading down a misdirected path.

At first, I didn't understand *how* I was to bless and pray for those who hated me and spitefully used me (see Luke 6:27-28). Even the Old Testament taught an eye for an eye and a tooth for a tooth (see Leviticus 24:19-21). What happened to God's judgment? What happened to God defending those who are His? I know this line of thinking may surprise you, but I didn't have a complete revelation of the new covenant.

> *Christ redeemed us from the curse of the law by becoming a curse for us, for it is written: "Cursed is everyone who is hung on a pole." He redeemed us in order that the blessing given to Abraham might come to the Gentiles through Christ Jesus, so that by faith, we might receive the promise of the Spirit.*
> Galatians 3:13-14 NIV

These verses explain that God defends the cursed under the new covenant. This new covenant runs counter to what many of us have been taught. If we curse someone, we directly oppose the very reason Jesus came and died. I believe this revelation was what the woman on the phone was also missing. We do not curse people, even if we think it's justified or seems right in our eyes. This matters significantly. God, by His very nature, will defend the one we curse even if they are not a good person.

> *With the tongue, we praise our Lord and Father, and with it, we curse human beings who have been made in God's likeness. Out of the same mouth come praise and cursing. My brothers and sisters, this should not be. Can both fresh water and saltwater flow from the same spring? My brothers and sisters, can a fig tree bear olives, or a grapevine bear figs? Neither can a salt spring produce fresh water.*
> James 3:9-12 NIV

While there are times I still may not know how to specifically pray for my enemies, I know I am called to pray. But not just pray, I am called to bless. How and what do I speak as a blessing? Many times, when I am at a loss for words, I will begin to pray in my spiritual prayer language and seek God's heart for an individual. I do the same thing when it comes to my enemies. I may not have the words, but God does. God knows His plans for us both. As I pray and wait, I know God will give me something to speak as a blessing. Sometimes is just as simple as, "God, I bless them to come into perfect alignment with all You have planned for their life." Sometimes, I may add a few other sentences like, "I bless them to know Your mercy and loving-kindness." Or "May they testify of Your goodness and Your favor."

Remember, God has a destiny for each person whether or not they are walking in it with Him. We must be careful not to curse others because it puts us in direct conflict and opposition to the entire reason Jesus sacrificed Himself. He did so for all, not just a select few.

Extreme Opposites

Blessing can quickly turn to cursing. It happens so fast. One minute we are in church praising God and worshiping Him for who He is. We hear a good sermon, participate in worship, and feel connected to God. Then, on the drive home, a car runs a red light, almost hitting us, or our spouse makes some sarcastic comment, or the kids start fighting, and we lose it. We no longer have praises or words of blessings coming out of our mouths. We don't just get upset but negative words, word curses, and the like flow from our mouths. It's too late to pull them back in, the damage is done. How quickly can our tongue get us in trouble? Very quickly!

> *Consider what a great forest is set on fire by a small spark. The tongue also is a fire, a world of evil among the parts of the body. It corrupts the whole body, sets the whole course of one's life on fire, and is itself set on fire by hell.*
>
> James 3:5b-6 NIV

When we curse others, whether intentionally or unintentionally, the damage is done and we come into alignment and agreement with the accuser, satan. As a believer, I do not want to be aligned at any time with the enemy or find myself in his camp. Like a tiny spark setting a forest on fire, so can the words we speak. We must be mindful and set a guard over our mouths, being willing and quick to repent when it gets the better of us.

We all stumble in many ways. Anyone who is never at fault in what they say is perfect, able to keep their whole body in check.

James 3:2 NIV

Not one person besides Jesus is perfect. We all have our moments and trip up. My stumbling is different from yours, but we all do it. When it comes to the words we speak, we will falter and mess up. Yes, we know God calls us to bless others, but in the heat of the moment, harsh words might come tumbling out. We can't take them back, but we can ask for forgiveness, put them under the blood of Jesus, and ask Him to heal the damage. We can also begin to speak and declare the opposite of the hurtful words spoken and release a blessing into and over the situation.

"But I say to you who hear: Love your enemies, do good to those who hate you, bless those who curse you and pray for those who spitefully use you."

Luke 6:27-28 ESV

The opposite of a blessing is a curse. God calls for us to speak words of blessing and life over those who curse us. It's the way we break the power of the curse. We move in the opposite spirit. A curse is darkness and death from the enemy's camp, while a blessing is light and life from the Kingdom of God. James 3 tells us how damaging our tongue can be.

Ironically, this same tongue can be both an instrument of blessing to our Lord and Father and a weapon that hurls curses upon others who are created in God's own image. One mouth streams forth both blessings and curses. My brothers and sisters, this is not how it should be.

James 3:9-10 The Voice

When we speak words, we align ourselves with either the kingdom of light or the kingdom of darkness. Gossip, curses, and slander are from the kingdom of darkness. Encouragement, praise, and blessing are from the kingdom of light. Light, life, and hope flow abundantly in God's Kingdom. Which kingdom have you been aligning your words with lately?

Growing up, I was labeled a loudmouth and a troublemaker. I had friends labeled as a "wild child," a "daredevil," or "the rebellious one." I would put these in the category of curses. While I may have been loud and outspoken as a child, I wasn't a loudmouth. I was always getting into trouble even though I hadn't done anything wrong, as I was the oldest and the one they could hear since my voice carried more than the others. I took the total weight of punishment while my sister and cousins often escaped. These "labels" we put on others are, in fact, curses and can cause exceeding damage. As an adult, I see how these labels became a part of my identity and even curses I spoke over myself. Maybe this has happened to you?

We must be careful when something negative is spoken about or revealed about an individual. If we begin to speak these things out, we are aligning our words with the power of darkness and releasing a curse. Don't worry though, there is hope. We can break the power of a curse and come out of agreement with it when we speak the opposite, which is a blessing. For example, we label someone as "rebellious" when they are challenging, strong-willed, resist authority or break the rules. Can you see how this might be a curse? Instead, what if we ask God for the truth and to show us the opposite of the spoken word curse? What is the redemptive quality of rebelliousness? Instead of negative terms, maybe we can use positive ones, such as, they are determined, straightforward, know their mind, or have a sense of justice and truth.

The enemy always wants to turn our strengths into weaknesses. He zeros in on our assets and does whatever he can to turn it into a deficit. For me, being a loudmouth was not a fun label and one I wanted to get rid of, so I shut my mouth. However, this didn't stop me from getting in trouble or being told I was loud because everyone was already speaking and proclaiming it over me. The strength of a loudmouth can be a variety of things, a teacher, an exhorter, bold, or outgoing. God has gifted me to be an exhorter and a teacher. As a child, I steered clear of both of these gifts because of the *loudmouth* curse over my life.

While writing this chapter and contemplating how blessings and curses are extreme opposites, I kept hearing the phrase, *"For every action, there is an equal and opposite reaction."* I knew it was a scientific theory, but I couldn't remember who said it and why the Holy Spirit kept bringing it to mind. So of course, I turned to google and had my aha moment. The Holy Spirit sure is the best teacher and imparter of wisdom. Sure, the phrase was part of Newton's law but how did it relate to blessings and curses?

Newton's third law is: For every action, there is an equal and opposite reaction.[50]

Meaning, if object A exerts a force on object B, object B also exerts an equal and opposite force on object A.[51]

If a curse is object A, then a blessing would be object B. Curses and blessings are the extreme opposite of one another and both are powerful forces. We see a cause and action or reaction. Newton's third law states, that forces always come in pairs, like curses and blessings.
The entire chapter of Deuteronomy 28 reveals blessings for obedience and curses for disobedience. There are consequences for our words and actions. In Genesis 1, God blessed Adam and Eve.

> *God blessed them and said to them, "Be fruitful and increase in number; fill the earth and subdue it. Rule over the fish in the sea and the birds in the sky and over every living creature that moves on the ground."*
>
> Genesis 1:28 NIV

However, just two chapters later, in Genesis 3:14-19, God proclaims curses over not just Adam and Eve for their disobedience, but He also pronounces a curse over the serpent who deceived them. The curses were a direct result of stepping out from under the blessing and choosing to disobey.

> *So the LORD God said to the serpent, "Because you have done this, "Cursed are you above all livestock and all wild animals! You will crawl on your belly and you will eat dust all the days of your life ...*
>
> Genesis 3:14 NIV

God continued to not only curse the serpent for several more verses, but He then condemns Adam and Eve for their actions. To quote Newton's law again: For every action, there is an equal and opposite reaction. Their disobedience demanded a response from God and brought on His curses and condemnation.

A curse can be reversed by blessing as well. We see this happen in 1 Chronicles 4:9-10 with Jabez. By all accounts, Jabez is a minor character in the Bible. There are only two verses regarding him in a long list of genealogy. The first nine chapters of 1 Chronicles is a list of names from the Hebrew tribes beginning with Adam and ending with Israel upon their return from captivity. In the entire nine chapters, no one else has more than their names listed except for Jabez. But why?

The account of Jabez plays an important role in demonstrating the power of blessings and what we can request from God. Jabez wanted God to reverse the curse he had been living under since the day he was born. Jabez may only be a minor player in the Bible but whole books have been written on his brief prayer request, what He specifically asked for and God's response.

> *Now Jabez was more honorable than his brothers, and his mother called his name Jabez, saying, "Because I bore him in pain." And Jabez called on the God of Israel saying, "Oh, that You would bless me indeed, and enlarge my territory, that Your hand would be with me, and that You would keep me from evil, that I may not cause pain!" So God granted him what he requested.*
> 1 Chronicles 4:9-10 NKJV

The name Jabez is *Hebrew for "he causes pain" or "he makes sorrowful"* as his mother stated, "I gave birth to him in pain." Bruce Wilkerson in his book *The Prayer of Jabez*[52] says, *"The word **Jabez** means "pain." A literal rendering could read, "He causes (or will cause) pain."* Jabez was labeled at birth with *pain* and *sorrow* also implying this would be his future, but he defied the odds and changed his predicted destiny. Jabez first became an honorable man and then a man of prayer. He knows God can reverse the curse spoken over him and cause blessing and abundance to be his new future, instead of pain. Jabez boldly cried out to God and his prayer changed everything. God granted his request! The same can happen with us.

Legacy Builders

Prayer

God, Your Word says, Your ways are not our ways and Your thoughts are not like ours. Forgive me for the times I have not remembered this. Forgive me when I want to judge others for what I think they deserve. Help me to remember You are working behind the scenes even when I can't see it. Forgive me when I misunderstood my place and spoke curses allowing darkness to thrive. I repent and ask that You would break the curses I have spoken and release Your life, love, and blessings in their place. God, I give You permission to continue to work on my heart and allow me to be an agent of blessing towards others, even those I perceive as my enemies. Amen.

Reflection

Can you think of labels that were put on you which are really a curse?

Are there curses that come to mind that you have spoken about yourself or toward others? If so, repent and ask God to give you the words to speak a blessing, replacing the curse spoken.

Is there a curse in your life that needs to be reversed? If so, what is it? And then write a blessing to cancel the curse and pronounce this blessing over yourself daily.

Blessing in Action

Write your own "Jabez" type prayer, requesting a blessing from God that is specific for you and your needs.

Chapter 9
Psalm 23 as a Blessing

*Bless those who persecute you; bless and do not
curse.*

Romans 12:14 NIV

As I neared the end of writing the previous chapter, on blessings and
curses, I felt the Holy Spirit quicken me to Psalms 23. At first, it seemed
like a strange thought that popped into my head, but I had just asked what
else I needed to include, so here we are.

Romans 12 tells us to bless those who persecute us. I am fairly sure
we could make a correlation with someone persecuting us as being our
enemy. If they are persecuting us, they are not for us, and we can see them
as the *enemy*. And if anyone knew about eating with the enemy or having
difficulties in life, it was King David. He penned a beautiful Psalm that is
probably one of the most well-known passages of Scripture in the Bible
and helps bring peace, comfort, and hope to those experiencing difficult
and trying times.

The Lord is my shepherd;
I shall not want.
He makes me to lie down in green pastures;
He leads me beside the still waters.
He restores my soul;
He leads me in the paths of righteousness
For His name's sake.

Yea, though I walk through the valley of the
shadow of death,
I will fear no evil;
For You are with me;
Your rod and Your staff, they comfort me.
You prepare a table before me in the presence of
my enemies;
You anoint my head with oil;
My cup runs over.
Surely goodness and mercy shall follow me
All the days of my life;
And I will dwell in the house of the LORD.

Psalm 23:5-6 NIV

I believe Psalm 23 is one of the most well-known passages in the Bible because it brings comfort and peace during difficult and trying times. Many can readily accept and even understand the truths in the first verses of Psalm 23. But verse five always seems to trip many of us up.

You prepare a table before me in the presence of
my enemies;

Psalm 23:5a NASB

If God is preparing a feast for us, He fully intends us to eat. Yet, how does one eat in the presence of their enemy? When face-to-face with the enemy, how does one bless and not curse? I don't know about you, but when I encounter an enemy, the furthest thing from my mind is eating and words of blessing are not on the tip of my tongue. I am on guard and do my best to keep a safeguard over my mouth as well. Truth be told, when confronted with an enemy, I am always looking for the nearest exit and planning my escape, should I need it. Have you ever found yourself seated at the table with someone you might consider your enemy? I did and it wasn't pleasant.

One evening, many years ago, my presence was demanded at a preplanned event right before I had given my notice to quit. The day before that phone call came, a blow-up erupted between myself and my boss. I was left feeling stunned having always considered her not only my manager but my friend.

96

As the phone rang, I glanced at the number on the caller ID. I groaned loudly and thought, *You've GOT to be kidding me!*

I considered not answering it and letting it go straight to voicemail but quickly decided against it. I figured I might as well get it over with, whatever "it" was going to be. Truthfully, after the hurtful accusations and hostile interaction with my boss the day before, I was surprised to be getting a call.

Logically I know people aren't the enemy, but in this situation, it sure felt like it. Especially emotionally. It felt like a line had been drawn in the sand and no matter what was said or done, all niceties were set aside, and war had been declared! We went from friends, ministry partners, and colleagues to all-out enemies in a matter of twenty-four hours.

It all started the week before. I had a hard, tearful yet agreeable conversation with my boss and she acknowledged God was moving me on to something else. There was a sense of sadness but also agreement that I was walking in obedience. However, a few days later and less than twenty-four hours prior to that phone call, a follow-up conversation turned into a war zone with word bombs hurled in my direction. Hurtful accusations were flying past my head at lightning speed. Many were untrue, but stung, nonetheless. I felt like I went from being a friend to a mortal enemy.

Have you ever been there?

It is not a fun place to be—no matter which side of the equation you find yourself on.

The phone call reminded me we had a pre-planned ministry dinner with others and my attendance was required, no *matter what*!

> *You prepare a feast for me*
> *in the presence of my enemies.*
>
> Psalm 23:5a NLT

I was dreading that meal and it felt like I would be eating with the enemy. I would like to say the dinner went well but it did not. My ministry colleague apparently had never been taught about airing dirty laundry in front of others. While sharing a meal with another couple (who were also our pastors) my boss, my husband, and I, made forward-looking plans for the ministry I would soon be leaving. It was a great, successful planning and brainstorming session. So much so, that I started to breathe a little easier and let my guard down. I thought maybe we could move forward past the last conversation, which was electrically charged with anger and hurt. That was until the business at hand was finished and the word formed, short-range missiles and ammunition fire began again.

Later during my quiet time, I was lamenting over the situation. I said to the Lord, "Thanks so much for preparing a table before me in the presence of my enemies—NOT."

The idea of having a table of food prepared for us to eat in the presence of our enemies is nice but when in war, sitting down to eat a prepared meal is the furthest from our minds. When in combat, you are on guard. You keep a watchful eye out for the enemy. When you eat, you eat in haste, not leisure. You may not see him, but you know he's there. When enemies are present, you keep your guard up, watchful eyes open, and ears tuned to every sound.

If we are honest with ourselves, we don't want to eat anything, let alone a feast with enemies around. Yet not only are we to eat with the enemy but we are also called to bless them and not curse them.

We need to dive into the wording to get a clear picture of what the Psalmist is saying.

> *You prepare a table before me in the presence of my enemies;*
>
> Psalm 23:5a NASB

- Prepare
- Table
- Presence
- Enemies

The original Hebrew word for **prepare** is *arak* and it means to: set in order; arrange; set in a row; ordain; or lay out.

The word for a **table** in the original text is *shulhan* and it literally means a table or king's table for private or sacred use; to set a spread or lay out a feast.

The phrase **in the presence of** means in front of, before me, in the sight of.

But who exactly is our enemy and adversary? The people who hurt us? Accuse us? Abuse us? Satan?

The **enemy** in this context means: adversary, be in affliction, besiege, bind up, be in distress, enemy, oppress, pangs, to be in straight trouble.

One commentator said the word **enemy** doesn't only mean a singular force like satan is against us. Instead, it's a more straightforward application. It's distress, pangs of trouble, oppression, affliction, etc.

Bible scholars form two general schools of thought about this particular verse. The first one, laid out in verses five and six, is a continuation of the "shepherd/sheep" metaphor from verses one through four. The second one proposed a switch that had occurred in verses five and six, no longer using the "shepherd/sheep" metaphor but instead is an allegory of God's relationship with His people. The switch comes when the verses shift from pointing to God as a shepherd to God as a host caring and providing for His people. An article on Psalm 23 from Encylopedia.com, points to a change that occurs from the first four verses to verse five.

> The metaphor for God shifts from shepherd to host. The role of host in most ancient civilizations was an important one. A host was obligated to provide his guests with comfort and pleasure, but he was also responsible for the protection of anyone staying in his house. God as host provides a table for a feast ...[53]

I can see it both ways. A shepherd's job is to lead the sheep to a food source. While they eat, the shepherd watches over and protects the sheep, knowing predators are always nearby.

> *You spread out a table before me, <u>provisions</u> in the midst of attack from my enemies;*
> Psalm 23:5a The Voice

Psalm 23:5a makes it clear that no matter what opposition, adversary, enemy, distress, or affliction is around, God will provide for all our needs. Even amid attacks and what feels like the enemy advancing or surrounding us, we can be at peace and partake of what the Lord so graciously provides for us.

> *You become my delicious feast even when my enemies dare to fight.*
>
> Psalm 23:5a TPT

We must take comfort that God will supply all our needs. He will provide a bountiful supply for us to feast upon in His presence and even protect us from our enemies. That is why He calls us to speak blessings and not curses. He tells us to pray for those who curse and use us spitefully.

> *You anoint my head with oil; my cup overflows.*
>
> Psalm 23:5b NIV

During the time of King David, it was culturally correct to anoint visitors with fragrant perfume and give them a cup of the best choice wine. This cup was filled to the top until running over. This was meant to convey a message and imply that while this individual (visitor) remained, there would be an abundance of everything they needed.

God is a God of overflowing blessings and abundance. He honors those who honor Him and longs to pour blessings upon us. The cup of blessing is not just full, it is overflowing. And David isn't writing about his cup overflowing once but it is a continual overflowing from God. As we live in the presence of the Holy Spirit and allow Him to flow through us, we will have abundant, consistent blessings. Scripture tells us those who follow the Lord will have rivers of Living Water flowing through them. It's a continual, never-ending flow.

> *Whoever believes in me, as Scripture has said, rivers of living water will flow from within them.*
>
> John 7:38

As we think about God's overflowing blessings, we must realize David isn't talking about material possessions or that nothing bad will ever happen. As you read David's story in the Bible, you can see he had plenty and lost plenty. You can see David had good times and experienced painful losses. But through it all, God provided for him, and He will do the same for us. God gives us more than what we need. God is generous and He wants us to be generous people. Not just with our finances but with our time, words, and actions. These things are blessings. He wants us to understand and walk in this because, as our cup overflows, we can overflow and bless others. Just like our Father, we can use what He has given us to be His blessing to others. Our words, spoken in blessing, form can be a powerful way to lavish and pour out His love to others.

> *Give, and you will receive. Your gift will return to you in full—pressed down, shaken together to make room for more, running over, and poured into your lap. The amount you give will determine the amount you get back.*
>
> Luke 6:38 NLT

Psalm 23 is not just a blessing David wrote to honor the Lord, it is a reminder of God's blessing and provision for us all. God calls King David a man after His own heart (see 1 Samuel 13:4; Acts 13:22) and He longs for us to be people who live and walk out Psalms 23. King David lived out what it means to be a Psalm 23 person and we can too. David isn't just writing poetic accolades towards God. The things David composed in the 23rd Psalm are heartfelt experiences. Yes, David experienced a table set before him in the presence of his enemies. God was faithful. He provided. He watched out for and guided David along the way. He honored David as His anointed King and as an individual. But most importantly, David came to understand that even his great sin and fears were no match for the love of God. God would always be there for him, and David had an open invitation to live, be, and dwell in the house of the Lord forever. That same invitation is there for us today.

I've thought about how I would paraphrase Psalms 23:5 to capture ALL it means. Here is what I came up with:

> *God arranges, in order, and lays out a spread for me. Not just any spread, but a feast fit for a King right in front of me and in sight of my adversaries and the things that cause me trouble, distress, and affliction. I can partake of His feast for me. I can*

"taste and see" the goodness and faithfulness of God all around me, no matter the situation. I can speak blessings over my enemy as I look them in the eye while eating a meal with them because I know I am not alone. God is guarding and watching over me, I choose to trust and rest in Him.

But more than that, we can turn all of Psalm 23 into a blessing we declare over ourselves and others. Just like the Aaronic Blessing in Numbers 6, Psalms 23 is a beautiful picture and blessing of a good and generous Father.

The LORD is my shepherd, I lack nothing.
He makes me lie down in green pastures,
he leads me beside quiet waters,
he refreshes my soul.
He guides me along the right paths
for his name's sake.
Even though I walk
through the darkest valley,
I will fear no evil,
for you are with me;
your rod and your staff,
they comfort me.
You prepare a table before me
in the presence of my enemies.
You anoint my head with oil;
my cup overflows.
Surely your goodness and love will follow me
all the days of my life,
and I will dwell in the house of the LORD
forever.

Psalm 23 NIV

Here are just a few examples of how we can turn portions of Psalm 23 into a blessing:

Verse 1: Because the LORD God is your/my shepherd, you/I will lack nothing.

Verse 3: May God guide you/me and direct your/ my path as He refreshes your/my soul.

Verse 5: May the Lord bless you/me and prepare a table before you/me in the presence of your/my enemies. May He anoint your/my head with oil and cause your/my cup to overflow.

Verse 6: May the goodness and love of God follow after you/me all the days of your/my life.

God not only wants us to know what Psalms 23 says but He wants us to live like a Psalm 23 person. To live as a Psalm 23 person, we need to understand that God is not just A good Shepherd, He is OUR good Shepherd. He is our best friend, and as a friend and a shepherd, He provides and cares for us, ALWAYS.

> *Yahweh is my best friend and my shepherd.*
> *I always have more than enough.*
> Psalm 23:1 TPT

Not only does God always watch out and care for us, but He also takes extra special care to ensure we can be free from fear and thrive in an environment of peace, refreshing, and rest. We can be fearless with God, and He causes our cup to overflow!

Legacy Builders

Prayer

God, there are individuals in my life I see as my enemies. I know I shouldn't, but I do. Please forgive me and help me to trust You fully all the time. God, help me to release blessings to those who persecute and curse me. I don't want to speak curses, but rather blessings. You are My Shepherd and My Best friend. Help me to fully understand and walk in this powerful revelation. As your blessings overflow in my life, show me how to bless others with my words and actions. Amen.

Reflection

What would it mean to live like a Psalm 23 person?

How would you write out Psalm 23:5 in your own words?

Does someone come to mind whom you might currently consider your enemy? If so, who? Now write a blessing to speak over them every time they come to mind or at least daily for a week.

Write out Psalm 23 as a blessing and begin to speak it over your life.

Blessing in Action

Choose someone in your life who needs a particular part of Psalm 23 spoken over them as a blessing in this season. Write it out and give it to them also speak it over them prophetically. *

* To speak prophetically, simply means to declare the blessing of the Lord by speaking it out loud. Remember, when we operate in the prophetic it is to encourage, comfort, and strengthen others. There is also a future-looking aspect to the prophetic which is different from just speaking something that is evident in the natural.

Chapter 10
Jewish Culture/Tradition

... I will surely bless you and give you many descendants.

Hebrews 6:14 NIV

Over the last seventeen years, I have thought a lot about blessings. In a way, I think I even romanticized them in my mind. In October 2007, just a few months after Graham Cooke spoke as the keynote at the very first Dare2Hear Conference, officially kicking off my formal ministry, I was invited to teach a workshop on blessings at one of his conferences in Vancouver, Washington. I was excited and knew it was a great honor and privilege to be asked to teach. I was so passionate about blessings and teaching people there was another aspect to the prophetic not being discussed or implemented in the church today. Everyone I talked to after the workshop had complimentary things to say and were encouraged by what I had to share. One woman said she had something that would help expand my teaching even more. She asked if I knew much about Jewish culture and how important blessings were to them. I didn't and said as much. She gave me her contact information on a piece of paper she tore out of her notebook. She included a few notes as well of other people I could contact for more research. I was excited.

Unfortunately, that piece of paper was lost, and I was unable to follow up with her. However, God in His great love for me had already made a way for me to talk with those who could point me in the right direction and speak to me from the viewpoint of Jewish culture and tradition.

Pastor Gary Fishman and Pastor Fred Rabinovitz have been gracious and incredibly helpful in unpacking this topic.

To say that what I came to learn surprised and shocked me is an understatement. What I discovered in my conversations with Jewish Christian believers and pastors caused me to change the title of this book from "Speaking & Pronouncing Prophetic Blessing" to "Legacy: Speaking and Pronouncing Blessings" to "Legacy—Releasing Prophetic Blessings" to finally, "Legacy: The Lost Art of Blessing." I will share more on the importance of the word **legacy** in chapter 16, "Leaving a Legacy", but just know this was God's word, not mine. I didn't fully understand it then but I do now.

What I learned from my conversations with Pastor Gary and Pastor Fred truly did astonish me. Before speaking with them, I had convinced myself the Jews had the market cornered on blessings. I felt talking with them would lead me to the key element I missed before and enable me to drive home the importance of Biblical blessings. I thought the Jewish people were continuing to carry forward this tradition today. Boy, I was in for a HUGE stunner. I had this idealistic idea the Jewish people were seeking God and asking Him for the words to speak and pronounce over their offspring to bring God's favor and blessing in their life. We have all watched movies portraying Jewish parents, especially the mother, as having big dreams and aspirations for their kids and constantly speaking positive pronouncements over them. OR maybe you had a Jewish classmate who was voted most likely to succeed in life and, in fact, did. Not only did they succeed, but they became wildly successful.

My line of thinking was simple: The Bible shows the people of God as blessed by God. It shows the people of God blessing their offspring and future generations. We see the power of the blessing in Scripture, and this is the heritage of the Jewish people. Therefore, it would still be a large part of their culture today. Before talking with anyone, my experience pointed to this line of thinking. And I even felt it should be taken one step further.

Here's my whole thought process: There is power in the words we speak; therefore, if we intentionally seek the heart of God and ask what He intends for a person to become and then speak over their life, it will happen. This means blessings are prophetic in nature and originate in the heart of Father God. When we intentionally seek Him and release these words of blessing over people, we are "marking" them in the spirit realm and asking God to put His favor on them and bless them.

This is what is modeled throughout the pages of Scripture with God's people, so it should be no different today. I assumed Jewish tradition and culture would continue this same practice. However, that is not exactly what I discovered. Maybe it was because many books and articles were written more than twenty years ago, and times have changed. The world I raised my children in is drastically different from the one we live in today. Many cultural traditions change over time and before we know it, something valuable and essential is lost.

I was excited to talk to Pastor Gary Fishman[54] so he could confirm what I believed to be a missing key element in the believer's walk today. Pastor Gary lives and ministers in the Bronx. He is a Jewish believer in Jesus who ministers with a heart for seeing a restoration of true New Testament Christianity. Gary's primary teaching emphasis is on understanding the Jewish roots of our faith and equipping the Body of Christ in prophetic gifts through classes, seminars, workshops, and conferences. Basically, he operates in the same vein and lane as I do, so I didn't need to explain where I was coming from with a prophetic bent. One initial conversation with Pastor Gary had my head spinning and made me rethink even authoring this book. The premise I had in my mind about the importance of the blessing in Jewish culture and tradition was going to be primary to my book, I thought. But in reality, it was anything but.

I asked an open-ended question of Pastor Gary about the importance of the blessing, even prophetic blessing, in Jewish culture and tradition and then let him talk. I furiously began writing notes. I didn't have time to let my heart process what I was hearing, but my mind was disappointed.

Pastor Gary explained what I was thinking wasn't really practiced anymore. He said there was a difference between the Biblical concept of blessing and the Rabbinical view. Today, in most Jewish homes, the parents say the priestly blessing starting with: *May God make you like Ephraim, and Manasseh/May God make you like Sarah, Rebecca, Rachel, and Leah,* and depending on whether the child is a boy or girl. In the synagogue, however, only a descendant of the high priest Aaron can say the actual priestly blessing. For instance, men with the last name Cohen[55] are thought to be descendants of Aaron. Today, there are actual DNA tests to reveal this heredity.

In Scripture, traditionally, the oldest child would receive the blessing, but today it is more of a blessing read over and released to the whole family, not just the eldest. Pastor Gary explained that a blessing today is more secular than prophetic in nature. Money and status are not the focus of blessing. Money is more of the method or mechanism a Jewish family will utilize to set their children up to achieve a successful, happy, and healthy life. Therefore, they are more motivated to discover what they can do to ensure their child will be happy, healthy, and prosperous. Part of that success is going to college and gaining influence; a byproduct of these things is attaining wealth.

The blessing today is more practical in action and application not just verbal. Yes, blessings leave a legacy, but parents want that legacy to also include health, happiness, and success because with that comes financial prosperity for their children. Parents are motivated to help bless their children however they can. They are even willing to refinance their homes if needed to ensure their children's education. Parents want their kids to have more and obtain more than they ever could.

Many modern families have limitations and mindsets that hold them back, but this is less likely to be true in many Jewish families. This mindset is not part of their history. Many Jewish families today don't want their children to have the restraints they did. They don't want their kids held back. These Jewish parents want their kids to surpass them and go farther. Essentially, they want their ceiling to be their children's floor and they are willing to sacrifice monetarily to do whatever it takes to make it happen and see their kids blessed. It's not that they are focused on money as much as they want their kids to be happy, excel, have more, do more, and accomplish more than they did. This is also true for most parents today. To me, the significant difference is that Jewish parents have a better understanding of the power and authority of the words they speak and the declaration they make over their children.

The blessing today in the Jewish culture is not just verbal, spiritual, or prophetic in nature but somewhat ritual. It's both spoken and shown. Much value is put on education, and it is spoken of often because they want their kids to excel. Parents reiterate in word and action their children will meet new challenges, but they will overcome them.

Pastor Gary also explained there are differences between Orthodox and non-religious Jews. While Orthodox Jews know about the Bible, their primary focus is on the rabbinical writings, the Talmud. Traditional Orthodox Jews don't necessarily study the Bible as we do. Instead, it's Rabbis who study Scripture and the congregation listens to and studies what their Rabbi says whether it be in written or oral form. Non-religious Jews, which are the vast majority, typically know little about Scripture so they wouldn't understand or necessarily see the importance of a Biblical blessing.

Pastor Gary went on to share with me about Leviticus 9 and Numbers 6, which confirmed what I was already teaching but he also gave more context and a fresh perspective. He pointed me to an article sharing how many Jewish parents today embrace the custom of blessing their children at the start of Shabbat on Friday evening. From our conversation and this article, I discovered parents lay their hands on their children's heads or sometimes cup their faces and speak the Priestly Blessing from Numbers 6 over them. while this can seem deeply personal and touching at first glance, it saddens me a little too. I think, for the most part, the Friday evening Shabbat blessing for children has become more of a liturgy. It's ritualistic in nature by the fact they are reciting by routine the blessing as something they are required to do as part of the Shabbat service. They lay hands on their children because it's what is expected of them, not because they are compelled to do so. It's simply, tradition and customary. Perhaps for some, it is deeply personal, and they are motivated by the desire to bless instead of blessing for the sake of expectations.

I needed time to process this. I felt there would be such a strong connection between what occurred in the Bible and how Jewish parents bless their children today. Maybe this portion of the book wasn't as important to God as I had thought. Perhaps I missed Him and spoken prophetic blessings aren't to be a legacy we impart to leave for our families and future generations. Maybe I had it all wrong and blessings, while they might be Biblical, weren't intended to be prophetic?

After marinating in what I learned, I knew I needed to reach out to someone else. I have known Pastor Fred Rabinovitz for over fifteen years. He is a Messianic Jewish believer and a fellow Foursquare Pastor. He's invited me to his church several times to preach and minister on Sunday mornings. He and his wife Melynda have always had a heart for giving people opportunities to minister. Pastor Fred even opened his church to me to hold a few Dare2Hear prophetic workshops and classes. I began by asking the same open-ended question I did of Pastor Gary and the conversation evolved from there.

We talked about the Friday night Shabbat liturgy blessings parents spoke over their children. He confirmed that like many Christians today, who defer their religious practices to the church, Jews tend to do the same and have deferred their religious practices and traditions to the synagogue experience.

From Pastor Fred's perspective, most non-orthodox Jews view blessings as a considerable part of their life and culture, just not in the way I had expected. He also confirmed what I had previously discovered; the Orthodox Jew is required to speak one-hundred blessings a day. The blessings acknowledge and reveal God is in everything. Their blessings cover everything from gratitude to blessing the food they eat and drink.

As a side note, I was curious about the different streams of Jewish religion both Pastor Gary and Pastor Fred referred to. I asked Fred to explain the difference between conservative Judaism (otherwise known as Masorti which is more mainstream) and Orthodox Judaism. He shared that just as Christianity has a variety of denominations and beliefs, the same is true in the Jewish faith. The main branches are orthodox, conservative, reformed, and reconstructionist. The Orthodox Jew is considered to be the most strict and dogmatic in keeping the rules and customs of the faith. In Conservative Judaism, they work for God's favor and don't believe they need a Savior.

Whenever I visited Pastor Fred's church, they took time to speak a blessing over the children before they released them to their Sunday School class. This was something unique to his church congregation and I hadn't seen it done in other churches where I had ministered before. I also wasn't sure if this was an identical prayer each time or if it was more Holy Spirit-led and prophetic. And I wanted to know why they did this. Was it because this was part of his Jewish heritage he wanted to bring to his congregation or something else?

"It is the right and important thing to do," he said. He felt the blessings were more spirit-led and while the words would change from week to week, blessing children was always incorporated during each service.

As the conversation progressed, Pastor Fred confirmed the book's title was indeed on target and God-breathed. I asked him to share his thoughts on the personal importance of blessings in his own life and the life of others. He felt blessings were extremely important and while he admittedly didn't say as many as he should, he believed blessings open portals to heavenly realms.

You may wonder what Pastor Fred meant by "portals and heavenly realms." I assure you that this is a very Biblical concept. We read an example of a heaven-to-earth portal and Jacob's ladder in Genesis 28. The dictionary describes a portal as a doorway, a gate, or an entrance to a place.[56] Candice Smithyman in an online article states, "From a spiritual perspective they (portals) are places that have been on earth from day one and we now have entrance to because of the death, burial, resurrection and ascension of Jesus Christ."[57] There are a variety of Scriptures that point to open heavens or portals from the beginning in Genesis all the way through to Revelation. In the story of the flood, in Genesis 7:11b we read ...

and the windows of the heavens were opened. (ESV)

And in Isaiah 64:1 we find...

Oh, that You would tear open the heavens and come down, That the mountains would quake at Your presence ... (NASB)

There are several other Biblical stories and Scriptures which point to this concept of heavenly realms and open portals. Here are just a few examples: Elijah taken to heaven (see 2 Kings 2:11), several in the Psalms (see Psalm 78:23-32; Psalms 144:5-15), Ezekiel's vision (see Ezekiel 1), Isaiah's vision (see Isaiah 6:1-4), Malachi's charge to test God in the tithe (see Malachi 3:10), Jesus' baptism (see Matthew 3:16), Jesus' promise to Nathanael (see John 1:51), Stephen's martyrdom (see Acts 7:54-610, Peter's vision (see Acts 10:11), and John's visions in several Scriptures (see 1 John; Revelation 4; Revelation 19:11).

Blessings are to be more than gratitude, thanksgiving, and praise. The power of the blessing may have lost some of its importance for us today, but they are vital since they are a part of God's character, nature, and intent for His people.

While Jewish tradition may not be what I initially thought it was, it did open my eyes. I discovered the spontaneous and prophetic nature of the original blessings seen throughout the Bible is a lost art. They have instead become more of a type of ceremony for many, spoken from custom. Blessings are powerful and important not just for today and every day after, but they are an essential part of the covenant God established with His people. If we receive the blessings God released over Abraham and Aaron and the blessings Joseph spoke over his children and grandchildren, then why wouldn't we continue this today? Why wouldn't we receive them and participate in them? What would it look like if we participated in releasing blessings to others? Would anything change and, if so, what? More on these questions later.

Legacy Builders

Prayer

God, thank You for revealing the power of the blessing in Scripture and its rich heritage for the Jewish people. Thank you for expanding my thinking, opening my eyes, and revealing this truth: Blessings were and still are an essential part of the covenants You establish with Your people. I now realize how important and powerful blessings are. I understand blessings are prophetic in nature and originate in Your heart, Father God. I choose to intentionally seek You and ask for Your help in releasing words of blessing and encouragement over people daily. When I do, I know You are "marking" them in the spirit realm, placing Your favor on them, and You will bless them.

Reflection

Did you learn anything about the Jewish culture and tradition that surprised you?

What are your thoughts regarding blessing children?

What are your thoughts about blessings opening heavenly portals?
What would it look like if we participated in releasing blessings to others? Would anything change and if so, what?

Blessing in Action

Choose three individuals whom you want to intentionally bless this week and speak a blessing over.

Now, seek God and ask Him to lead you to a Scripture or to show you a picture or a word to base your blessing on. Then write out each blessing and contact the individual and speak the blessing directly to them. Once you have done this, give them the written copy as well.

Chapter 11
Why Speak Blessings

Do not repay evil with evil or insult with insult. On the contrary, repay evil with blessing, because to this you were called so that you may inherit a blessing.

1 Peter 3:9 NIV

At the end of a teaching session, I looked around the room, spotted the clock and quickly surveyed the class. My eyes were drawn to one woman. I pointed at her and said, "God's not finished with you yet. There is plenty of time left for you." She immediately burst into tears.

I had just finished a workshop at a church in Wyoming and was about to dismiss for lunch. Before I did, I challenged the class to speak a word of encouragement to their lunch server. I promised it wasn't difficult. Building on an "items in a bag" activation exercise we had just finished, I instructed the class to find an object in the restaurant and speak a word of encouragement based on that item. To give an example, I chose an item, the clock. Then I chose the person I felt God was directing me to speak over. I was not expecting the instantaneous crying. I quickly said a prayer, dismissed the class, and approached the now sobbing woman I had just ministered to.

I simply stood quietly by while several people consoled her. One of her friends turned to me and explained that she had just received a cancer diagnosis. I was shocked, out of all the people in the room, God had chosen her to receive an encouraging word regarding time. *All right God, I thought to myself, what are you up to?* I proceeded to quietly wait and pray while the woman composed herself. By now, the room had emptied for lunch except for those of us on the teaching and ministry team and the handful who had stayed behind to console the women.

The woman shared with me she had just learned of her diagnosis and the doctors didn't give her much hope for a future. Her family and friends had been seeking God's plans for her and praying for a miracle.

Yes, God, I thought, *what are Your plans for her?* He nudged my heart and said, *I already spoke about my plans when you released the word. I now want you to pray for her and bless her with long life and health.*

Bless her? I thought that was strange but okay. I didn't know much about blessings at the time, as this was years before I began intensely studying the subject. However, what I did know was how to hear God's voice and obey. So, I prayed with her, encouraged her, and blessed her just as God asked me to. God knew what she needed. She had been asking God how much time she had left and if He was done with her on earth. He answered it and then some. What an honor and privilege to be a part of God's answer.

Just as I modeled that day in Wyoming, speaking words of blessing and encouragement does not have to be difficult or complicated. Sure, we can prepare and craft blessings in advance to speak over another but sometimes we may need to be spontaneous. The preparation and experience we get from crafting blessings in advance help us when moments of spontaneity are required.

My first attempt at speaking a blessing left me feeling extremely nervous. I was in a grocery store, and I know I bumbled over my words. I wasn't eloquent but it did catch the cashier's attention. I quickly and softly said, "May you be surprised by God today."

She gave me a confused look. "Did you say God was going to surprise me today?" I just nodded my head yes. "Why would God want to surprise me?" she quizzed.

"Because He's good and He knows you like surprises. Have a great day," I blurted out as I rushed away with my cart.

She remembered me the next time I came in. She didn't know it, but I purposefully chose her line, even though it was long. This is what I call "marketplace ministry," ministry that happens when you are out and about living life and encounter people who need a touch from Jesus. She was now going to be *my cashier* no matter how long a line I had to wait in. I fully intended to bless her again. But with what?

I decided to take what the marketing gurus planned as a way to increase their profits and turn it around for good to benefit others. I spotted a pack of skittles, and this gave me the idea of crafting and pronouncing blessings over her and even over those standing in line with me.

When thinking about crafting or spontaneously speaking a blessing using candy, I think about their slogans or ads.

- **Skittles:** Taste the rainbow of flavor.
- **Double Mint Gum:** Double your pleasure, double your fun with Double Mint Gum
- **Peanut Butter Cups:** Two great tastes that taste great together

Once you are drawn to a particular person and candy item the fun begins in fashioning a blessing. There is no right or wrong way and crafting a blessing may look something like this:

- **Skittles:** The word *rainbow* stands out to me, and rainbows remind me of promise. So, I am going to craft a blessing around that word.
  - ° No matter how things may seem, God's promises over you are still true.
  - ° God is true to His word and His promises over your life will come to pass.

- **Double Mint Gum:** The words *double* and *fun* stand out to me so I will ask God what He has to say to the individual based on those words.
  - ° May you experience the fun, joyous side of God. He loves to laugh and is extending an invitation for you to laugh with Him.
  - ° May the works of your hands be doubly

blessed and favored by God.

- **Peanut Butter Cups:** The words *great togeth-er and taste* stand out to me,
  - ° Much like a peanut butter cup, you and God are two great things that go well together.
  - ° God is inviting you to "taste and see how good He is." May you experience the good-ness of God in new ways throughout this year and beyond starting today.

I think you get the idea, but it doesn't just have to be items in a grocery store. It can be a tattoo, a piece of jewelry, or their piercing blue eyes. It can be the clock, a picture, or even a saltshaker. God can give you blessings and words of encouragement regarding just about anything if you make yourself willing and available.

This is exactly what I did with *my cashier* at the grocery store. While I didn't yet have the revelation to use candy during my first encounter, I simply asked God for one word I could quickly fashion a blessing from and share directly with her. The word He gave me was "surprise" and I had the sense she liked surprises. The blessing was simple: "May you be surprised by God today." It hit the mark and opened a spiritual door for the Holy Spirit to go to work and for me to continue interacting with her.

Why Speak a Blessing?

We are called to bless others and in return, we will receive or inherit a blessing. In 1 Peter, the Bible is clear in saying we are directed to bless no matter what our ministry calling or profession is.

> *Do not repay evil with evil or insult with insult. On the contrary, repay evil with blessing, because to this you were called so that you may inherit a blessing.*
>
> 1 Peter 3:9 NIV

The simple fact is we live in a negative world. In his book *Bless and Be Blessed*, Peter M. Lord states: "We live in a very negative world, where negative things have power and prominence."[58]

120

He also asks us to think about the impact it has on our society:

- When an authority calls you, do you expect rebuke or commendation?
- Has a police officer ever stopped you and thanked you for driving safely, courteously, or for staying in the proper lane, etc.?
- What do teachers mark on school papers? The wrong answers.
- Have you noticed that if you do a hundred good things and one bad thing, it is usually the wrong thing that is remembered or mentioned?[59]

I don't know about you, but when the police have pulled me over, it wasn't to thank me for stopping at the stop sign. My teachers were forever marking my papers with their blazing red pens to brightly highlight my wrong answers. Most often, when an authority calls you into their office, it isn't good news. And, finally, yes … I can relate to doing more than one hundred things correct, over-the-top stellar in fact, and yet when I mess up, it's the one error everyone remembers.

I used to work as an administrative assistant in the Worship Arts Department of a large church before I got my pastoral license. It wasn't because I played an instrument or sang but rather because I couldn't. The current pastor said she was tired of hiring people who were part of the church worship team because their attention was split and they always wanted to focus on the music side, not the administrative side. She needed someone to focus solely on the administrative side and I was a perfect fit. I loved my job and working with her.

However, one time we were away at a women's conference our church was hosting and one of the camera people couldn't make it. I was asked if I would run the camera and I emphatically and rather forcefully said, "NO." I reminded everyone I was challenged when it came to technology. I was the worship arts admin because I didn't do any of the worship arts "stuff." Running a camera was something that fit into that category of "stuff" and was not admin related.

When they still couldn't find someone, they returned with a convincing proposal. I could run the camera in the front row, it would be super easy, just follow the speaker, no need to zoom in or out. They told me I could have a friend or two sit with me to sweeten the deal. You guessed it, I ended up saying yes and having a grand time. I had front-row seats and very minimal work to do with the camera.

The keynote speaker was legally blind, so she didn't move far away from the podium. Okay, except for the one time she got very close to the edge of the stage and everyone who could see her collectively gasped. Operating the camera was going so well that I asked one of the tech people to show me how to zoom in and out and some of the more advanced tricks. I was feeling pretty confident … that is until our senior pastor spoke. She moved a lot. She was not tied to the podium, and I had to pay closer attention. But I was still doing pretty well, and I even started zooming in for effect when she said something important. One might say I was a little overconfident in my ability and wasn't as focused as I should have been.

The pastor had stopped, and I was framing her perfectly with a Ficus tree right behind her. She proceeded to give a Scripture reference and then quoted the verse. It was the wrong reference. I knew it. I turned to my friend and said, "she's got the incorrect reference, quickly find out what it should be." Then I heard the murmurs. I thought to myself, *oh no, how embarrassing for her, everyone else knows she gave the wrong reference too!* But that wasn't why they were whispering. I literally took my eyes off her for maybe three to five seconds, and when I looked back up at the camera lens, she was nowhere in sight. But the Ficus tree was still perfectly in the frame!

I quickly located her on the stage and swiftly moved the camera to her location. Then laughter erupted. Not only had I just given everyone motion sickness but the worship team and my friends sitting in the front row with me laughed the loudest. One of the worship leaders leaned forward and through tears streaming down her face, told me that was the funniest thing she had witnessed in a long time. I did not think it was funny at all, especially after being continually reminded about it. And it didn't stop there, they kept it up for a long while.

That one mistake caused me so much angst. My friends, on the other hand, got mileage out of it for years. No one cared I had stepped in to help operate the camera when they had no one else. No one cared that I ran the camera perfectly and even started to apply some of the more difficult techniques almost the entire weekend. Nope, all they cared about was the moment I messed up.

We do live in a world where negative news stories dominate. No one wants to hear about the cute little cat the firefighters rescued from the tree. No, they want to hear the nitty-gritty details of all the awful things happening in the world. It's sad, but bad news is king.

The year 2020 brought many gloomy and divisive words into the atmosphere. Not only did we deal with a worldwide pandemic, but it was also a heated political year. Well, when is a political year not heated? But seriously, 2020 did not bring out the best in society. It pushed our buttons and boundaries of normalcy. It caused many to get angry, overwhelmed, and loud. There is always noise we must filter through but in 2020 there was an excessive amount and, in many ways, the noise has continued to intensify in the years after and is still prominent now.

At any given time, we must filter out the noise to hear the voice of truth. However, there are times like 2020 when there is so much noise it's difficult to find a moment of peace and silence. In many ways, the words spoken in and around the pandemic of 2020, and the years that followed, were negative and some may have even crossed into word curses. Scripture is clear. We are to speak words of life and not death. Proverbs 18:21 tells us our words are powerful, and with them, we can either bless or curse. This will affect all areas in our life if we're not careful.

> *The tongue can bring death or life; those who love*
> *to talk will reap the consequences.*
> Proverbs 18:21 NLT

> *Speak blessing, not cursing, ...*
> Romans 12:14a TPT

The opposite of a blessing is a curse. If we aren't speaking words of life, hope, and blessing then we are speaking the opposite. The opposite are words of death, despair, and curses. I don't imagine we think of it like that. I believe most of us speak words but don't fully understand the power, magnitude, or weight they carry in the spiritual realm. In his book, *The Power of the Spoken Blessings*, Bill Gothard says, "Death and life are in the power of the tongue. Our words have the power to crush or to heal, to break bones or to plant a tree of life where none has grown before."[60]

Words have power when they are released. Let's make sure we speak words of blessing and life, not death and destruction.

> *Our words are so powerful that they will kill or give life, and the talkative person will reap the consequences.*
>
> Proverbs 18:21 TPT

Jesus says that we are to be the light and salt on the earth (see Matthew 5:13-16). We are called to shine light in the darkness to reveal the truth of God's Word. We are to rise above negativity and expose lies by speaking the truth of God in love. We were never meant to dwell or focus on the negativity surrounding us. Instead, we are to be the salt that adds flavor to this world. We are called to share the truth of the Gospel message of hope, life, and love. We are to speak blessings and not curses. We are to love like God loves and in the way Jesus modeled. The love of God is pure, holy, and righteous; we are to live in His love and dwell on these things (see Philippians 4:8).

> *Love is patient, love is kind. It does not envy, it does not boast, it is not proud. It does not dishonor others, it is not self-seeking, it is not easily angered, it keeps no record of wrongs. Love does not delight in evil but rejoices with the truth. It always protects, always trusts, always hopes, always perseveres. Love never fails.*
>
> 1 Corinthians 13:4-8a NIV

Legacy Builders

Prayer

Holy Spirit, help me to be the light and salt of the earth Jesus intends me to be. Show me how to rise above the negativity swirling around and expose any lies I have been believing. Awaken and heighten my spiritual discernment to know Your truth. Help me filter the noise in the spirit realm so I can attune my ear to hear Your voice more clearly. Allow the love of God the Father to emanate from me with every word I speak and action I take. With Your help God, I want to bring healing to hurting people and restoration to broken relationships starting in my own life. I know I can only do this if I learn to love as God does. Help me to live and love according to 1 Corinthians 13. Amen.

Reflection

Is there something negative in your life you are remembered for?

What *noise* do you have to filter through to hear God clearly?

What does it mean to you to be light and salt in the earth?

What does it mean to you to love as God loves?

Meditate on 1 Corinthians 13:4-8.

Blessing in Action

Think about someone in your life who tends to be negative. Write out a blessing or word of encouragement and speak it over them. Continue to pray this blessing or word over them daily for a week and then note how their attitude or behavior changes.

Chapter 12
How and Whom We Bless

The LORD said to Moses, "Tell Aaron and his sons,
'This is how you are to bless the Israelites.
Numbers 6:22-23 NIV

By this point, hopefully, I have convinced you how important blessings are. But I am sure you are curious and even anxious to learn how we begin to bless others.

Before we jump right into the "how to's" there is something else we must understand.

There are many types of blessings and blessings for all occasions that can be imparted to others. But for the most part, they fall into two categories— blessings for the present moment and blessings for the future.

Present blessings are simply blessings that speak to a person right where they are. They are living eulogies we speak to others, pointing out what character traits and qualities are present and those we see that may be hidden. Present blessings are visible and true. It's similar to speaking words of affirmation, love, and kindness to someone for something they have done or are currently doing. As Peter M. Lord says, "We call attention to what is noteworthy in them."[61]

A *present* blessing is more like a word of encouragement and would look something like this:

- You are always so joyful whenever I see you.
  ° God created you to be filled with much joy.
- You are tenderhearted and generous with your time and money.
  ° God gave you the gift of generosity to go with your tender heart.
- You always see the good in every situation.
  ° The ability to see the good around you is a gift from God.
- You create a pleasant work environment filled with excellence and I appreciate your thoughtfulness and consideration in the workplace.
  ° God gifted you with amazing leadership skills to provide a peaceful work environment that is filled with excellence. He has given you a caring and thoughtful heart to care for those you lead.

In a world full of negativity, we want to speak positivity to others. We want to call out the hidden gold shining like a bright light. Everyone has positive and negative qualities, actions, and character traits. There may even be negative qualities or actions that far outshine the good ones. We must not focus on these negatives but instead call out and point to the good. This will release life and open spiritual doors for them to receive the love and kindness of God. And it has the potential to transform and heal their wounds and negative mindsets.

Blessings for the future are prophetic in nature. They speak to the potential of what someone can or will do later. Hebrews 11, also known as the "Hall of Fame" for faith chapter, includes two specific mentions of those attributed to speaking blessings by faith prophetically (see Hebrews 11:20-21). They were not present blessings but rather for the future, drawing out the untapped potential as they perceived it. Peter M. Lord says it this way: "We can give prophetic blessings when, under the leadership of the Holy Spirit, we see the potential in others and tell them about that potential."[62] He goes on to say these blessings can be general or specific.

A *general* future blessing might look like this:

- May you be surprised by the goodness of God today.
- Just as the rain refreshes and revives the land, May the Lord revive and refresh you.

While a general *person-specific* future blessing could be:

- With your creativity and artistic talent, you will be a great interior designer one day.
- May the Lord richly bless your creativity and artistic talent to earn a living doing what He has gifted you to do.

Also, a specific *future* blessing is when you intentionally and specifically seek God through prayer and ask Him to reveal something about how He views another and what His plans are for them. An example of this type of specific future-looking blessing would be precisely what we see both Isaac and Jacob doing when they blessed their children and grandchildren. Scripture specifically references Isaac blessing his sons concerning things to come.

> *By faith Isaac blessed Jacob and Esau concerning things to come.*
>
> Hebrews 11:20 KJV

I have specifically asked God what His plans and purposes were for my children, and I wrote or crafted blessings around them so I could read them over my kids and pray into them. I also like to do this for the babies and children of others as well as newly married couples. I will often write these blessings in cards so they can have them for future reference.

One such example is a personal one concerning my son Jesse. Jesse was always a compliant, thoughtful, quiet child. He was easygoing and often went with the flow. He was comfortable serving and helping others or going along for the ride.

However, the Lord showed me when Jesse was little he had a leadership calling and a heart like King David, especially when it pertained to worship. So, I blessed this in Jesse every chance I got. I prayed over him and blessed the leadership call on his life. I prayed he would be a man after God's own heart like King David and that he would not just be a worshipper of God but would use his musical gifts to bless the Lord and others.

When Jesse was little, he would bang on pots and pans with a spoon but there was no real inkling of musical talent or gifting in him for some time. When he was in the fourth grade, he asked to play the violin at school because it was the only instrument they had instructions for. I would love to tell you my son was a musical genius on the violin but alas, he was not. There were times when I would cringe at the sounds that poor violin made when he practiced. That year was rough in our household but thank Jesus for earplugs! Jesse then switched to saxophone when he could join the school band, but it wasn't until he began to take private lessons for bass and electric guitar that I saw the fruition of the blessings I had been speaking over him since he was little. Today, as an adult, I can confidently say Jesse has grown into a leader. He is also a man after God's heart and worshiper like King David. He regularly plays on the worship team at his church, and it brings this momma's heart much joy when I watch.

One crucial element for speaking these future types of blessings is faith. In fact, Hebrews 11:20-21 explains that a future blessing includes a faith aspect.

> By **faith** Isaac blessed Jacob and Esau concerning
> things to come.
> By **faith** Jacob, when he was a dying, blessed both
> the sons of Joseph; and worshipped, leaning upon
> the top of his staff.
> Hebrews 11:20-21

When we ask and listen to the Holy Spirit, we must *by faith* begin to declare these blessings.

> Now faith is **being sure of what we hope for and
> certain of what we do not see.**
> Hebrews 11:1

By faith, we declare what God has shown us or spoken to us for another. We get these types of prophetic blessings by spending time with God. When I began blessing my son with leadership abilities and a worshipper's heart, they were not evident. I, *by faith* declared and prayed what I believed God had shown me. Watchman Nee, in his book *Release of the Spirit*, states, "God will back and bless whatever he initiates."[63] More on this statement later, but we have also learned from Numbers 6:24-26 that God backs what He says. This occurs when we add the name of the Lord to what we speak, *I will bless them.* (Numbers 6:27)

If God backs the blessing He initiates, why wouldn't we always ask Him what He wants to speak to an individual at the coffee stand, the grocery store, or the bus stop? Just like when we say, "God Bless You," when someone sneezes, we add God's name to what we have said and intentionally ask Him to bless them. We don't have to make it super complicated or even churchy. When I teach classes on this, I make it fun and let people be creative. Don't worry, you will get to experience these activation exercises in a later chapter.

As you look at the difference between the present and future blessings, I pray you can see the power added when we make these pronouncements more spiritual in nature. In my opinion, we need to put more emphasis on having blessings flow from our spirit rather than our soul (mind, will, and emotions). Plus make them more about what God wants or intends to do in the future and not just in the present. Kick it up a notch to flow from the spiritual and future-looking position.

> *... The spirit is willing, but the flesh is weak.*
> Matthew 26:41 NIV

The book *Blessing Your Spirit* by Sylvia Gunter and Arthur Burk discusses the importance of blessing our spirit and the spirit of others. Our spiritual identity is where we need to operate from, not our soul. We have all experienced trauma and wounds as we have journeyed through life. Our spirit is the perfect part of us created by God to connect with Him on a spiritual level.

> A person's spirit should rule the soul, but it doesn't
> get there automatically or accidentally.
> ~Arthur Burke[64]

I mean, let's be honest. Do you want me ministering to you out of my flesh (body), soul, or out of my spirit?

> *Now maybe you're learning: the spirit is willing,*
> *but the body is weak. Watch and pray and take*
> *care that you are not pulled down during a time of*
> *testing.*
>
> Matthew 26:41 The Voice

During my eight-week training on hearing from God, I first build a solid scriptural foundation. One of the first topics we discuss is how we are made in the image of God (see Genesis 1:26-27). God is a three-part being, Father, Son, and Holy Spirit, and so are we. We have a body, soul, and spirit.

> *May your **whole spirit, soul and body** be kept*
> *blameless at the coming of our Lord Jesus Christ.*
>
> 1 Thessalonians 5:23b NIV

Our bodies are fearfully and wonderfully made (see Psalm 139:13-14) by God and given to us while we live here on earth. The soul is our mind, will, and emotions and our spirit is how we commune and communicate with God. God breathed His *pneuma* breath into us. Our spirits are what sets us apart from other living creatures. It is of the utmost importance that we operate from our spiritual identity, especially when we minister.

> *You were taught, with regard to your former way*
> *of life, to put off **your old self**, which is being*
> *corrupted by its deceitful desires; to be made new*
> *in the **attitude of your minds**; and to put on **the new***
> ***self**, created to be like God in true righteousness*
> *and holiness.*
>
> Ephesians 4:22-24 NIV

To live life in the Spirit, we need to understand God's basic design for us. The Word of God explains to us how we are made and how we are to function. In Ephesians 4:22-24, three distinct parts are defined:[65]

> ***Your old self*** – refers to the body.
> ***Attitude of your minds*** – refers to your soul.
> ***The new self*** – refers to your spirit.

I further explain what it means to operate and minister from our spirit and ask which they would prefer me to operate from. Debbie (the body) is 5'5 inches tall with blonde hair that comes from a bottle. Debbie is extra fluffy, overly tired, and her eye color changes depending on what she's wearing. Most often, Debbie's soul just wants to stay home in her comfy clothes to watch an absorbing movie or read an intriguing mystery book. However, Debbie (the spirit) loves God and loves people. She is a child of the Most High and a daughter of the King. She understands that NO weapon formed against her will prosper and that Jesus has given her the keys to the kingdom to set captives free.

I jokingly ask people, "Which identity of Debbie do you want to minister to you?" Obviously, the answer is the spirit. Trust me, you want me to step over into the spirit when ministering and hearing from God, otherwise, you may get a soulish word that isn't a word from God at all.

That doesn't mean the present, soul realm blessings are bad. For my birthday one year, a friend wrote over fifty single words, covering my birthday card. These single words were virtues and character traits seen in me. Words like loyal, honest, loving, courageous, and more. It was one of the best birthday gifts ever. I still have it. It's a great encouragement and a reminder of what others see in me.

I like to think of the natural level of blessing as something most of us already do, but we aren't necessarily aware of it. They pack a powerful spiritual punch when we add the spiritual element of looking to the future. I like to think of it working together like a one-two punch combination … in a good way, of course.

Peter M. Lord states, "The difference between the natural and spiritual eulogy is not worth worrying about since it is very hard to make a mistake eulogizing anyone."[66]

As we focus on loving God and loving others, I am confident He will bless our efforts even if they come from natural wisdom. I firmly believe that as our focus is on God and we partner with Holy Spirit, He will give us thoughts and ideas we may not be conscious are from Him. I have a lot of great and good thoughts, which are not always God's ideas, but He blesses them nonetheless. I am confident He will do the same for you.

How We Bless

I am a show-me-how-to-do-it type of person. So, when I first developed my teaching on speaking and pronouncing blessings, you can bet I had an activation exercise to go along with it. Part of learning is receiving instruction through reading, seeing, or hearing. But another part of learning is the practical application of what you learned. I am sure you have heard individuals quoting specific statistics around learning retention. Such as this one, from Edgar Dale in an online education, document titled *We Remember*:

> 10% of what we read 20% of what we hear 30% of what we see 50% of what we see and hear 70% of what we discuss with others 80% of what we personally experience 95% or what we teach others.[67]

However, many have a tough time believing you can accurately assess a specific percentage of retention. One such website boldly refuted this by stating: There is no scientific evidence to back up the percent-remembering numbers.[68] And another stated: People do NOT remember 10% of what they read, 20% of what they see, 30% of what they hear, etc. That information and similar pronouncements are fraudulent.[69]

As a teacher, it would have been nice to have concrete proof of statistics and percentages. However, whether the statistics are accurate or incorrect, I know one thing for certain, I am more likely to retain something if I do more than read, hear, or see it. If I can "do the stuff," then I will be more likely to understand it and continue to implement it in my own life. Therefore, I like to use props as a jumping-off point when I teach. It helps in kickstarting the realization that ideas and thoughts really do come from the heavenly realm, even when beginning in the natural. That is the way God works. Everything need not be super spiritual.

God speaks to people in numerous ways, but we often discount things that come to mind as our thoughts and not God's. I have found that I may have a thought but if I am walking in the spirit and connected to the Spirit of God, then His thoughts *are* my thoughts. Yes, He gives me thoughts that are smarter than anything I could ever come up with on my own. I call these God's thoughts. God's thoughts are those brilliant ideas you can't produce on your own, no matter how hard you try.

To help activate individuals when it comes to speaking a blessing, I start them out by asking them to find a blessing in the Word of God to speak over themselves and personalize it. We've already discussed Numbers 6 and Psalms 23, but many more are found throughout Scripture.

My mother is especially good at finding a Scripture or a spiritual topic and writing a blessing from it. It all began when she attended a conference and was challenged to choose someone who would become her blessing partner. My mom was attending with a group of women, so they each paired up. Afterwards, my mother and her friend would call each other weekly and leave a blessing on each other's voice messages. They planned to work through the fruit of the spirit one year at a time. Their styles differed because of their personalities but the blessings were still powerful and effective. My mom added her grandkids to the weekly messages and when I complained I was being left out, she added me as well. My mom had to stop when my dad became sick, requiring more time to care for him but she had been doing it for two-and-a-half years. I will share more of her story in chapter 16 and the basics of how she crafts her blessings.

What makes a blessing a blessing, not just kind or thoughtful words?

I am so glad you asked. It has to do with learning to hear God's voice. You may have an object like a watch or a phone in the natural, that you utilize as your starting point but when you ask the Holy Spirit to partner with you, it moves from the natural to the Supernatural.

Blessings can be private or public proclamations, however, I feel they must be spoken boldly with authority and confidence. A verbal blessing is made up of three things:

- Our words
- God's Word
- God's name

An example of this would be: *As you stand at a crossroads of decision, may God guide and direct your path. May He refresh your soul, not just today, but every day.* Which is taken from Psalm 23:3. This uses God's Word, His name is attached to it, and we have also added our own words too. You can ask God for a specific Scripture that would be meaningful to the individual. When you add your own words, I highly recommend praying and asking God to share specifically what He would like you to speak to make it personal for the individual you are blessing.

When we seek to hear the Father's heart for an individual, He will give us the words to speak. Anytime God speaks, it will always line up with Scripture, His character, and His nature. If it does not, then it is not God. Blessings are proclamations using our words, God's word from Scripture, or what we feel, sense, or hear Him speak and will also have God's name attached to it.

> *The LORD bless you and keep you;*
> Numbers 6:24 NIV

In Chapter 6, when we broke down Aaron's blessing, we looked at seven powerful things a blessing can do when you speak and pronounce it. For a quick recap, they were:

1. Give Favor and Protection
2. Be pleased
3. Be Merciful and Compassionate
4. Give His approval
5. Give Peace
6. God's Name
7. God Blesses

God wants to bless us!

> *and I will personally bless them.*
> Numbers 6:27 NLT

He wants His name attached to words of encouragement and blessing. Attaching His name to our blessings grants the Holy Spirit access to move on behalf of those receiving the blessings.

What should we do?

We need to be a beacon of hope in a negative world. We must remember when we speak, our words significantly affect us and those around us. Good words spoken to us meet even the most basic of needs. Peter M. Lord says, "Good words spoken by significant people in our lives are essential. However, good words can come from other sources, and regardless of who speaks them, they be a blessing."[70]

> *"It is written, 'Man shall not live by bread alone, but by every word that proceeds from the mouth of God.'"*
>
> Matthew 4:4 NKJV

God's Word comes to us directly through the Bible, or it can come in the form of a prophetic word or blessing from others.

God's Word tells us what to do in Hebrews 3:13

> *But* encourage one another day after day, *as* long *as it is still* called "Today," so *that* none *of you will be* hardened *by the* deceitfulness *of* sin. (NASB)

God the Father was our example. He bestowed a blessing upon Adam and Eve, Abraham, and the Children of Israel in Numbers 6. But He also bestowed a verbal public proclamation over Jesus in Matthew 3:17.

> *"This is My beloved Son, in whom I am well pleased."* (NKJV)

When was the last time you deliberately praised or blessed someone?

Peter M. Lord, in his book, *Bless and Be Bles*sed, says, "We need to remember the darker the night the brighter the light—our positive words and attitudes will stand out in a world of negativism.*"[71]*

Remember, James 3:2-11 teaches us just how powerful both blessings and curses can be.

> *... But no man can tame the tongue. It is an unruly evil, full of deadly poison. With it we bless our God and Father, and with it we curse men, who have been made in the similitude of God. Out of the same mouth proceed blessing and cursing.*
>
> James 3:8b-10a NKJV

Finally, the Word tells us: "We are to worship without ceasing—blessing God continually because of who He is ... (see Revelation 4:11; Revelation 5:12)."

If we live from our spiritual identity, then blessings should overflow to those around us. Here are several suggestions so you can get started.

- Start by blessing your family:
    ° Spouse, children, parents, and so on

- Next, bless those people at church whose work is often overlooked:
    ° Greeters, ushers, janitors

- Then begin to speak blessings to those you meet at work, in the grocery store, and at restaurants. Ask God what He wants to speak to a person and deliver it in a safe package—a blessing.

In some ways finding who to bless is easier than figuring out how or what to bless them with. If we're honest we all want to receive a word, encouragement, or blessing. Everyone is a potential target to receive a blessing. To begin releasing blessings to others, you just need to start by first asking God who and then what He wants to speak to them. The *how* can be based on a Scripture or He can give you an object, a word, or an impression as discussed in previous chapters. An important part of the *how-to* is to be a willing vessel God can use to speak through, then to listen for what He has to say, and finally begin to bless others. There is no formula, but the steps are as easy as 1, 2, 3 ... BLESS!

1. Be Willing
2. Ask God who to bless
3. Listen for what God speaks
4. Write it down or speak it spontaneously
5. Release blessings to others

Legacy Builders

Prayer

Heavenly Father, help me to be a beacon of hope and a bright shining light pointing toward You. Show me how to be a treasure hunter and discover the hidden treasure and gold you have placed in others. Help me see past the negative or bad in them and see their God potential.

I want to bless others with heavenly words that will make a lasting impact and not only speak kind or thoughtful words. Release the Holy Spirit to teach me how to bless others by faith in a future-looking prophetic way. Amen.

Reflection

Are you convinced how important blessings are?

What do you think about this statement: "God backs the blessing He initiates?"

What have you done in your life that God would say you did "*by faith?*"

How can you be a beacon of hope?

Blessing in Action

Think of someone whose negative qualities or actions come to mind before their positive ones. Ask God to show you the hidden treasure and gold inside of that individual. Write a blessing for this, calling out their hidden gold, and give it to them.

139

Chapter 13
Prophecy

Follow the way of love and eagerly desire gifts of the Spirit, especially prophecy.

1 Corinthians 14:1NIV

If you know me, you know we can't talk about blessings without talking about prophetic encouragement. It's at the core of who I am and how I am wired. The topic has been interwoven throughout the book, but I think it's an important and integral part of blessing, so it needs to be brought to the forefront for a moment. I know some who are reading this book may not know what the prophetic is or understand its importance today. I also know there are those who may not have even read my other books on the prophetic. I don't want to be one of *those* authors who say, "go read my other books." Truthfully, that is a pet peeve of mine. However, sometimes it's necessary to point people to other valuable resources to expand their knowledge and understanding on a particular topic. I only have one chapter in this book to discuss the importance of prophecy and how it's tied to blessings. Prophetic encouragement aka prophecy is so important that I have written an entire book on this topic called, *The Gift of Prophetic Encouragement: Hearing the Word of God for Other*s. You can check it out if you want a more in-depth teaching and understanding. For now, I will do my utmost best to give you the highlights in this chapter.

Follow the way of love and eagerly desire gifts of the Spirit, especially prophecy. For anyone who speaks in a tongue does not speak to

141

people but to God. Indeed, no one understands them; they utter mysteries by the Spirit. But the one who prophesies speaks to people for their strengthening, encouraging and comfort. Anyone who speaks in a tongue edifies themselves, but the one who prophesies edifies the church. I would like every one of you to speak in tongues, but I would rather have you prophesy. The one who prophesies is greater than the one who speaks in tongues, unless someone interprets, so that the church may be edified.

1 Corinthians 14:1-5 NIV

The spiritual gift of prophecy is for all. Paul wants us to eagerly desire this gift which means it is for everyone. I am not talking about being a prophet or having a mantle of prophecy but simply hearing from God. As we read 1 Corinthians, there are several things we must understand.

First, we must operate in love when we use any of the spiritual gifts. Paul not only starts chapter 14 out with the charge to "Follow the way of love and eagerly desire spiritual gifts, " but the entire previous chapter, 1 Corinthians 13, is dedicated to LOVE … including what love is, what it isn't and what we are like when we are not operating in love. Next, everyone is wired to hear from God. It's our destiny, our God-given design, our inheritance. It's who we are and how we were made to function from the very beginning.[72] This is a challenge for us all to Dare2Hear the voice of God and to take hold of the truth so we can hear from Him. We first begin to access this truth as we read the Word of God.

> *My sheep listen to my voice; I know them, and they follow me."*
>
> John 10:27 NIV

My definition of the spiritual gift of prophecy is from John 5:19-20 and John 10:27. The prophetic and prophecy is: The ability and willingness to hear God speak to us, speaking it out, and then obeying it![73]

God longs for His people to use the gifts He has given them, especially the gift of prophecy. The spiritual gift of prophecy is speaking Holy Spirit-inspired words of edification, exhortation, or comfort to individuals.

Prophetic encouragement is something every follower of Christ can give to others in their day-to-day life. This simple truth opens our eyes to the ordinary nature of prophecy to breathe life, love, and hope into the dry places of our lives.[74]

One of my favorite portions of 1 Corinthians 14 is found later in the chapter and correlates beautifully with the opening chapter of this book regarding blessing having the potential to open spiritual doors for the Holy Spirit to intentionally target people for good. Prophetic encouragement and blessings have the power to open people's eyes to the truth of God and reveal that He is not only real but that He knows them personally.

> *But if an unbeliever or an inquirer comes in while everyone is prophesying, they are convicted of sin and are brought under judgment by all, as the secrets of their hearts are laid bare. So they will fall down and worship God, exclaiming, "God is really among you!"*
> 1 Corinthians 14:24-25 NIV

I am not an evangelist by nature. I would feel awkward and out of place standing on a street corner or on a box in the middle of the town square proclaiming the good news of the Gospel. Even when preaching on a Sunday morning, my bent was not toward the salvation message and sinners' prayer. Not that it isn't important or needed, but my strength is in other areas like hearing God, exhorting, and calling individuals up to a higher level and standard. I can give, and have given, an alter call and salvation messages before, but honestly, it's not my strength. That is why my husband and I flow so beautifully together. He has a true father's heart for people and has no problems wrapping up a service with an invitation to walk away from selfish ambition, sin, and fleshy desires to join the Kingdom of God.

However, this does not absolve me from sharing the good news and evangelizing those I meet or who are in my sphere of influence. We are all called to be ourselves and share our testimonies of what God has done for us. If I am being myself, I will encourage and exhort others. And that means I'm going to hear what heaven has to say regarding people and I'm going to share it. I've seen the power of a prophetic word spoken to an unbeliever in the marketplace and church buildings. I have witnessed firsthand individuals repent (fall down) and begin to worship God, exclaiming, "God is really among you!" (see 1 Corinthians 14:25).

In my book, *The Gift of Prophetic Encouragement*, I state: "Prophetic messages are more than validation, reassurances, or knowledge of what the future holds. God longs to breathe life, hope, and healing into the lives of His children through the gift of prophetic encouragement. He wants us *all* to be available to speak His words to those we meet, regardless of their relationship with God."[75]

By asking God for the words, we should speak (prophecy), we release His heart and intentions toward others. A prophetic blessing can directly impact a person specifically. Most blessings today seem general or generic in nature ... a one-size-fits-all, if you will. However, that is not what God intends them to be. By speaking the very heart of God prophetically, an additional powerful layer to blessings is added that are sadly missing today. Thus, they are a lost art, if you will. Blessings alone are powerful. They open spiritual doors and can make a long-lasting impact but by adding an element of the prophetic to a blessing, it takes it to the next level. Or, as Emeril Lagasse would say, "Let's kick it up a notch." Whenever possible, blessings can and should have a prophetic element to them. They are not just mere words of encouragement we speak, declare, or impart to others. They can be the very words that originate from the heart of our heavenly Father, they are the power of the blessing itself.

To add a prophetic element to blessings, I encourage you to start by asking God to give you a picture, word, or impression. When He does, ask Him to then give you a Scripture and the words. This is the process I used for the example I gave from Psalm 23:3 in chapter 12. As I asked the Lord what He wanted me to write, He gave me a picture of someone standing at a crossroads. A choice needed to be made. Then the Holy Spirit impressed me with the Scripture, and I began to write a blessing based on what God was showing me and speaking to me, giving me the resulting blessing:

As you stand at a crossroads of decision, may God guide and direct your path. May He refresh your soul, not just today, but every day.

Legacy Builders

Prayer

Jesus, You modeled perfectly what it means to follow the way of love and walk in spiritual gifts. Show me how to do the same. I want the words I speak to others not just to be mere words of encouragement but to be powerful prophetic words of encouragement. Words that will transform hearts and lives to walk in Your Kingdom's purposes. I want to be trustworthy by walking in the truths You reveal to me. Holy Spirit teach me how to do this correctly. God, hearing from You is part of my inheritance and destiny. Awaken the prophetic in me and tune my ears to hear God's voice more clearly. Amen.

Reflection

What are your thoughts regarding the prophetic?

Have you ever received a prophetic word? How did it make you feel?

Have you ever given a prophetic word of encouragement to someone?

Blessing in Action

It's time to kick it up a notch. Ask God for the name of a family member or friend who is not a believer and write out and give them a prophetic blessing or prophetic word of encouragement.

Chapter 14
Prophetic Blessing

Anxiety weighs down the heart, but a kind word cheers it up.

Proverbs 12:25 NIV

Blessings are kind, good words spoken and pronounced over individuals with the intent that God would bless them with whatever is spoken and released. Blessings by themselves are powerful and highly effective, but when they are prophetic in nature, they have the authority and power of heaven backing them up.

If you recall, my simple definition of prophecy is hearing God speak and then responding in obedience to what He says. Prophecy finds the hidden gold locked away in individuals and calls it forth. We all have buried treasure; gifts, skills, and talents others see in us but for whatever reason, sometimes we cannot see them in ourselves. God will use prophecy to validate and uncover hidden gifts, and even release others into His plans. Blessings can be simple and spontaneous or carefully crafted. The prophetic aspect of a blessing is what brings potential power and Godly authority to unlock and release this hidden treasure.

We see many of the blessings in the Bible were originally spoken spontaneously but it doesn't mean they weren't also thought and prayed about. I believe just as Isaac sent Esau to prepare his favorite meal, readying himself to receive his father's blessing, that Isaac was planning too (see Genesis 27:1-4). Scripture doesn't specifically say how Isaac

147

knew what to say as a blessing to his son. But I do believe that while he sent Esau away to prepare, he was also praying, contemplating, and asking God for exactly what blessing he should release.

> *"May God give you of the dew of heaven*
> *and of the fatness of the earth*
> *and plenty of grain and wine.*
> *Let peoples serve you,*
> *and nations bow down to you.*
> *Be lord over your brothers,*
> *and may your mother›s sons bow down to you.*
> *Cursed be everyone who curses you,*
> *and blessed be everyone who blesses you!"*
> Genesis 27:28-29 ESV

I think the same is true with Jacob when he blessed his grandsons Manasseh and Ephraim in Genesis 48. He spontaneously spoke prophetically over each boy. He was listening to what God was asking him to say and then he said it. He even blessed the younger with the blessings the oldest child should have received. Jacob didn't just decide to do this on his own. I believe God directed him in the moment. He continues to speak over all his sons in Genesis 49.

> *And Jacob called his sons and said, "Gather together, that **I may tell you what shall befall** you in the last days: "Gather together and hear, you sons of Jacob, and listen to Israel your father.*
> Genesis 49:1-2 NKJV

When Jacob spoke over his sons, he used both information in the present as well as prophetic God-given information. Jacob had natural knowledge to pull from when it came to his sons' lives. But I also believe it was prophetic in nature because Jacob could not know in advance what would happen in the future to his sons, but God did. Therefore, God revealed that to him prophetically.

Today, we see that Jewish culture isn't necessarily spontaneous when it comes to blessing as their predecessors were. It is more by rote and recitation of Scripture. Don't get me wrong; there is nothing amiss with reciting Scripture or memorizing and recounting a prayer of blessing.

However, I think if we just do this alone, we are missing a very key element regarding the character and nature of who God is and how Jesus lived His life. When we partner with Heaven, as Jesus did, and seek the heart of the Father as to what a blessing should be, we are flowing prophetically. Jesus only did and said what the Father did and said (see John 5:18-20; John 12:49), this is prophecy in action. We need to imitate Jesus and do and say only what Jesus does and says. Blessings can be spontaneous at the moment, or they can take more time as you write them out and carefully craft them.

This prophetic nature of blessing others is truly a lost art God wants us to redeem.

In the previous chapter, I shared my thoughts regarding prophecy and its importance today. If you don't know much about prophecy, I urge you to read up on it and explore just why it's so important and I believe necessary. The spiritual gift of prophecy is to encourage, comfort, and build others up. It's what proverbs would call a "kind" word cheering others up.

> *Anxiety weighs down the heart, but a kind word cheers it up.*
>
> Proverbs 12:25 NIV

What would it look like if we intentionally set out to encourage and bless those we meet?

Market Place Ministry

When I first learned to step out and prophetically minister to people, the church seemed the safest place to learn. But my previous pastor, Jerry Tyler, challenged me by exhorting God had more. An entire world outside the church needed a touch and a glimpse of a loving God who knew them by name. Pastor Jerry was not only my pastor, but he also sat on my ministry board. He taught at many workshops and conferences I held or facilitated over the years. His teaching style was relaxed, and always packed a punch filled with revelation. Throughout the Scriptures Jesus modeled for us how we are to live our lives. There are many examples of marketplace ministry that seemed ordinary throughout the Bible, yet they radically changed people, cities, and whole areas from one prophetic encounter.

One of my favorite marketplace ministry messages Pastor Jerry frequently taught at our prophetic workshops and seminars was on the woman at the well. If you recall, I mentioned that I'm not an evangelist by nature. But something about the way Pastor Jerry presented the story of Jesus ministering to the woman at the well ignited a spark deep within me. As I already confessed in chapter 13, I don't see myself as an evangelist. Quite honestly, prior to hearing Pastor Jerry teach on marketplace ministry, I never gave it a second thought. But his teaching birthed a passion in me that could only come from God. It connected with my heart in a way that hadn't happened before. 1 Corinthians 14 talks about the effect prophecy can have in marketplace ministry in a roundabout way.

> *But if an unbeliever or an inquirer comes in while everyone is prophesying, they are convicted of sin and are brought under judgment by all, as the secrets of their hearts are laid bare. So they will fall down and worship God, exclaiming, "God is really among you!"*
>
> 1 Corinthians 14:24-25 NIV

These verses specifically talk about what happens inside the church when an unbeliever hears a word of prophecy, yet I knew it could be just as effective outside a church setting. Not just effective but necessary because there are many who will never cross the threshold of a church. But we as individual members of the church are the church, and we encounter them in our day-to-day activities. After hearing Pastor Jerry's message and processing it with him, I knew what God had called me to use my gifting both inside and outside the church building.

To the casual observer and even the disciples, Jesus had an insignificant conversation with a woman at the well. But it was so much more than that. She was Jesus' assignment that day. The disciples didn't get it, they didn't even stick around to find out why Jesus decided to stop at the well and sit for a spell. They had hunger on the brain and went into town in search of food and completely missed witnessing a powerful encounter that changed not only the woman's life, but an entire community. She was seeking truth, but until she encountered Jesus, she wasn't finding it.

Searching for Truth

People are searching for truth and are hungry for the supernatural of God! In the quest for answers, they may be drawn into the world's idea of the supernatural and before they know it, they're trapped. Many people we meet may have beliefs that don't align with ours. Yet they still need answers that the world can't give them. But you and I as Christ followers can.

I don't know about you, but I often fail to speak to others about my beliefs because I feel, or rather assume, they won't be interested. But that is not always the case. Many individuals go through life starving because of unanswered questions or partial answers. We as the church have the food (answers and solutions) they are looking for.

As you read story of the woman at the well in John 4:1-42, you will see Jesus chose to stay and rest as his disciples went to look for food. As He rested by the well, a woman approached to collect water at midday which was unusual. It was hot at that time of day and most drew water in the cooler parts of the day, she was intentionally avoiding whomever she could because of her reputation. What was more unusual, is that Jesus spoke to her. In those days, it was unheard of for a Jew to speak to a Samaritan. What followed was a significant prophetic encounter that not only impacted the woman but the community and the entire region.

When people encounter the living God, they are forever changed. No matter how good or messy their life is, things are radically different when they're touched by the reality of a real and personable God.

Touched by the Prophetic

How did one conversation open a whole region?

The woman at the well was profoundly touched by a prophetic word and she went on to tell everyone she encountered. She opened the door for the town to come and see Jesus. When Pastor Jerry would speak on this, I loved that he often said, "Having been touched by the prophetic, she became prophetic to her town."

I knew this encounter at the well was part of how God wanted to utilize

151

me. I didn't have to make some grand show and state God had a message for someone about something. I could have casual conversations with the people I met and impart spiritual truths, blessings, prophetic words, and, yes, even prophetic blessings.

Remember I said I felt the church was the safest place to step out in the prophetic? Well, Pastor Jerry's teaching challenged and dared me to step out. I still wasn't confident in my ability to speak prophetically to others, and quite honestly, operating in the marketplace seemed overwhelming and somewhat scary. Yet, I knew Jesus started by asking for a drink of water, using the very thing she was there for. He then listened to His Father in Heaven for what He wanted to say to her. I figured I could do the same thing as well. When I struck up conversations with others or someone began one with me, I learned to tune my ear and ask Father God what He might want to say to them. I would inevitably feel impressed to share something I knew God was giving me. I just worked the revelation and truth into my casual conversation, releasing the prophetic over their life. Sometimes it would be a word of knowledge, a picture, a scripture, or even a blessing.

One ministry night, I was sharing my excitement with my friends and one of them laughed and said, "Debbie, we need to call you the drive-by prophet!" I must have had a puzzled look on my face, so he elaborated. "People are getting a "drive-by" when they are in conversation with you. They don't realize it, but you release blessings and prophetic words that make an impact, and they don't know what just hit them. All they do know is they walk away feeling good after encountering you." This made my heart happy. I want to be a blessing to others. I want to speak truth and life and impart hope. I want to live as Jesus did.

I know you may not see yourself as prophetic and if you have ever been around anyone who is, you may compare yourself to them. DON'T! Please, don't compare yourself to anyone. You are unique and carry what God wants you to carry. The world and God need us all to be about His business.

You may be curious to know how exactly the woman at the well story, and Jesus ministering to her prophetically, relate to speaking and pronouncing blessings. It's simple. You may never give a prophetic word to someone and that's okay. But you can give a blessing. The important takeaway from this story is that Jesus was open to going where His Father directed Him and was willing to speak what God told Him to say.

Can I let you in on a little secret? I'm not fearless. Not even close. Every time I start a conversation, intending to minister prophetically or bless someone, there is a part of me that is afraid. I can push fear aside more easily today but it's still there. Before having a history with God and His faithfulness, I worried and was often overcome with fear. I was afraid of rejection and saying something wrong. Now I have a history of God faithfully showing up. I've realized it doesn't matter how people respond, I just need to be obedient. I'm a big proponent of the "just do it afraid" motto. I'll let you in on another little secret, sometimes I wrote the blessings out I spoke over people before I met them. I asked God in advance for a Scripture or a prophetic word I could share with someone I would meet that day. I didn't want to "freeze" from fear, so I wrote these things down on pieces of paper and carried them in my wallet to grab at a moment's notice. I am happy to report I don't need to do that now but if I did, it's a tool I can utilize.

Let's make it a point to be open to the things of God so we can operate in our sphere of influence. When we do, let's remember to walk with humility and wisdom as we meet people. It's all about Jesus and allowing them to encounter Him. We can do that by purposefully speaking blessings that will open spiritual doors for the Holy Spirit to bring God's delight, goodness, love, and favor. We must have the courage and willingness to obey what God wants to do through us so the world around us will change.

Legacy Builders

Prayer

Heavenly Father, give me wisdom as I live my life and interact with people who may not yet know You. I want to be obedient to hearken to the sound of Your voice. I want to say what You say and do what You show me. You have not given me a spirit of fear, so I ask You to remove it from my life. I am your child and I have Your Spirit living within me. Allow me to daily follow in the footsteps of Jesus. Give me the courage, boldness, and willingness to obey You. May others see You in my life and may they encounter Jesus in a real and tangible way. Amen.

Reflection

Do you have people in your life searching for truth?

Has fear ever stopped you from obeying God?

Do you compare yourself to others? If so, ask God to remove this spirit of comparison and ask Him to show you your worth and value.

Do you see yourself as prophetic?

How can you use prophetic blessings to touch people in the marketplace?

Blessing in Action

It's time to kick it up another notch. Speak a spontaneous prophetic blessing over someone in the "marketplace." A barista, store clerk, server, etc.

Chapter 15
Types of Blessings

Man shall not live on bread alone, but on every
word that comes from the mouth of God.
Matthew 4:4 NIV

As you can imagine, there are many distinct types of blessings we can begin speaking. I was surprised to learn that according to the Talmud, an Orthodox Jew should speak one hundred blessings daily. They have a specified number of blessings to speak in the morning, afternoon, and evening. These are blessings of thanksgiving, they cover everything from food and drink to leaving the bathroom, going to sleep, and everything in between.[76]

An online article titled *100 Blessings,* from March 2020 stated, "For an Orthodox Jew who prays three times a day, this is fairly easy to accomplish. One hundred blessings are about cultivating the awareness that is the foundation of radical love and joy."[77]

It might be difficult for us to imagine speaking quite that many but at the same time, God does call us to speak blessings every day, all day.

While I was thinking through the several types of blessings, I was fully aware the list I pulled together in this chapter is not inclusive. Just as God speaks in many ways to His people, there are also many opportunities and ways we can bless ourselves and others. I'm sure you will have more to add to the list, which is terrific. Feel free to do that. I chose to highlight the ones I have participated in that incorporate life cycles or are talked about in Scripture.

They are:

1. Blessings from Scripture
2. Blessing Children
3. Wedding Blessing
4. Baby Blessing
5. Blessing Leadership
6. Blessing of Victory
7. Blessing of Health and fruitfulness
8. Prosperity
9. Plus, many more

Blessings from Scripture

God's word is powerful when we just read it but when we declare it over our life and situation, there seems to be an extra measure of power. I believe as we use our voice to speak the Word of God with power and authority, there is exponential power unleashed. God's Word is alive.

> *For the word of God is living and powerful, and sharper than any two-edged sword, piercing even to the division of soul and spirit, and of joints and marrow, and is a discerner of the thoughts and intents of the heart.*
>
> Hebrews 4:12 NKJV

Scripture already contains many blessings, promises, and covenants from God. We can speak these over our life and watch God do miraculous things. But also, we can take any verse in the Word of God and fashion a blessing from it that is just as powerful. In each of the sections below, I will give an example of a Scripture and a blessing you can pray over others and yourself.

Blessing children

Children are special to God. Jesus modeled this very thing and showed us we are not just to love children, we are to become like a child if we want to receive the Kingdom of Heaven.

> *He said to them, "Let the children come to me. Don't stop them! For the Kingdom of God belongs to those who are like these children. I tell you the truth, anyone who doesn't receive the Kingdom of God like a child will never enter it." Then he took the children in his arms and placed his hands on their heads and blessed them.*
>
> Mark 10:14-16 NLT

Children play a significant role in the Kingdom of God and are a gift from God. We can be a part of blessing His children not only as parents or grandparents but as spiritual parents. A blessing spoken to a child can remind them they are loved and seen.

> *Blessing children accomplishes much more than merely encouraging them in the daily lives.*
>
> ~ William T. Ligon, Sr.[78]

When blessing children, we can speak to their true identity in Christ and create shields of protection around them. Blessings, like prayers, can be given anytime but here are a few ideas to help get you started. Start the day by blessing your child or bless them at bedtime. Bless them on their birthday or special holidays and everyday in-between.

In his book *Imparting the Blessing*, William T. Ligon says, "No one can place a value on your children. They are priceless gifts from the Lord. ... Satan sees covenant children as the greatest threat to his plans. He does not want children to come under the covenant blessings of God."[79]

When blessing children, I do my best to ask God for specific details He would like me to include so each one is different and unique. Here is a sample blessing based on Proverbs 3:4 and Proverbs 22:6:

- May you grow in favor with God and man. I declare you will have a solid foundation which is built upon Jesus Christ. As you grow older, may you retain the wisdom and knowledge imparted to you from Scripture and your parents. You shall not forget what you have been taught.

Wedding blessing

These are blessings spoken over the bride and groom at a wedding ceremony and can be given before or after the ceremony. I have been present at weddings when a special time was set aside during the ceremony for specific individuals to release prophetic blessings over a couple. I have written blessings and included them in my card. Also, as a minister when performing a wedding ceremony, I specifically ask God for a blessing I can release over the couple during the ceremony.

The Traditional Jewish wedding ceremony includes seven blessings that are a key element. These seven blessings are called the Sheva Brachot. The seven blessings are adapted from ancient rabbinic teachings, beginning with the blessing over the wine and ending with a communal expression of joy.[80]

In many ceremonies, the Sheva Brachot prayers are read or chanted in both Hebrew and English. There are also numerous modern English variations on the blessings. The traditional Hebrew transliteration (A *transliteration* is the process of transferring a word from the alphabet of one language to another. *Transliteration* helps people pronounce words and names in foreign languages.[81]) and English translation of the Seven Blessings/Sheva Brachot follow:[82]

1. Blessed are You, Adonai our God, Ruler of the Universe, Creator of the fruit of the vine.

2. Blessed are You, Adonai, our God, Ruler of the universe, Who has created everything for your glory.

3. Blessed are You, Adonai, our God, Ruler of the universe, Creator of Human Beings.

4. Blessed are You, Adonai, our God, Ruler of the universe, Who has fashioned human beings in your image, according to your likeness, and has fashioned from it a lasting mold. Bless-

ed are You Adonai, Creator of Human Beings

5. Bring intense joy and exultation through the ingathering of Her children (Jerusalem). Blessed are You, Adonai, are the One who gladdens Zion (Israel) through Her children's return.

6. Gladden the beloved companions as You gladdened Your creatures in the garden of Eden. Blessed are You, Adonai, Who gladdens this couple.

7. Blessed are You, Adonai, our God, Ruler of the universe, Who created joy and gladness, loving couples, mirth, glad song, pleasure, delight, love, loving communities, peace, and companionship. Adonai, our God, let there soon be heard in the cities of Judah and the streets of Jerusalem the sound of joy and the sound of gladness, the voice of the loving couple, the sound of their jubilance from their canopies and of the youths from their song-filled feasts. Blessed are You Who causes the couple to rejoice, one with the other.[83]

What better way to establish a solid foundation between a couple than to begin their marriage covenant with the intended blessings of God.

I have had the honor of presiding over more than a few wedding ceremonies and I always love to end each one with a spontaneous prophetic blessing. Each one is different and unique to the specific couple. Sometimes, I will intentionally ask God in advance to craft a prayer tailored specifically to the couple and write it in their card. Here are a few generic examples:

- Our prayer and blessing for the two of you is that you will continue to grow in love... love for one another, love for God, & love for your neighbor.
- As you have just pledged your faith in, and love to, each other, may God grant you a deep abiding love for one another. May He abun-

dantly bless your marriage and ever increase your love.

Baby Blessing

Just as Jesus was brought to the temple after His birth to be dedicated, we do much the same in modern Christianity with baby dedications. A denomination or a church's liturgy will depend on when this occurs. For Jesus, it happened just eight days after He was born. You can read the entire portion in Luke 2:21-40.

> *Simeon was there. He took the child in his arms and praised God, saying, "Sovereign Lord, now let your servant die in peace, as you have promised. I have seen your salvation, which you have prepared for all people. He is a light to reveal God to the nations, and he is the glory of your people Israel!" Jesus' parents were amazed at what was being said about him. Then Simeon blessed them ...*
>
> Luke 2:28-34 NLT

While you may not be a pastor or ministry leader who will formally dedicate and bless a newborn baby, you can do it in other ways. Write a blessing in the card you give at a baby shower. Take time to speak blessings over the child and mother. Make special arrangements to speak and impart a blessing over the baby.

Blessing babies is much like blessing children. Again, I ask God for specific details He would like me to include so each one is different and unique. Here is an example of a generic baby blessing:

- As you grow into who God has designed and created you to be, may you always cling to Him. May you always know you are the apple of His eye. May your spiritual eyes and ears be attuned to the sounds of your Father in Heaven. As you grow may you learn the sound of His voice and be filled with His wisdom and peace.

Another type of blessing I like to fashion for babies and even children is around their name. This type of blessing is powerful. First, I determine what the meaning of their name is and ask God to speak prophetically to me regarding His purpose and how it associates with their name. I have a favorite baby name book that has the inherent meaning of a name and also the spiritual connotation with a Scripture reference. I firmly believe God has a hand in naming us and our children far more than we know. Yes, our parents may have named us, but God is the instigator behind it.

Take me for example. My name is Debbie, not Deborah. My mom wanted to call me Darcy, but my dad was insistent I be called Debbie. My mom attempted to persuade my dad to call me Deborah because that was a good Biblical name, but he wasn't having any of it. Growing up I hated my name. I hated its meaning, which is "honeybee." Out of all the animals I would want to associate with my name, a bee was not one of them. For one, my dad was deathly allergic to bee stings and after living the trauma of watching him almost die from one as a small child, I never understood why he wanted to name me after a bee! Not to mention they have oddly proportioned bodies and were not glamourous like peacocks, or fascinating like elephants or fearsome like tigers. I didn't like the names my mom wanted either but if I had to be a Debbie, I wish they would have at least let me legally be a Debra (yes, not the Biblical spelling) and call me Debbie. I didn't want the Biblical spelling because I had read about her in the Bible. I wanted nothing to do with her and didn't like it when people would compare me to her. I have since gotten over that.

It wasn't until I was in my thirties that I came to truly appreciate my name and understand God had a bigger role than I knew in choosing my name. I have a couple of ministry friends who set up tents at outreach events like fun days and festivals. We used to partner together often to offer dream interpretation and "spiritual readings" aka prophetic ministry. Our church was hosting a back-to-school event for children, and I invited my friend to set up her tents. Because it was an event for kids, she invited a mutual friend to join her to help out with a fabulous activity for children based on their names. She had a business that formed a family's spiritual tree using each member of the family's name and its spiritual meaning. She would create a spiritual roadmap of the family's influence, calling, and destiny. It was at this event one of my ministry team members designed a name tag for me, implementing what we were doing in the tent. Basically, we would look a child's name up in a baby name book and write a prophetic sentence summarizing what their name meant, combined with what God was showing us. My name appears like this in my baby name book:

Deborah, Deb, Debb, Debbi, Debbie, Deborah,[84]
(and several other spellings of the name):
Language/Culture origin: Hebrew
Inherent Meaning: Honeybee
Spiritual Connotation: New Era of Leadership
Scripture: Isaiah 65:17

I have only ever heard of the meaning of Debbie as: Bee. Deborah was the Biblical prophetess who summoned Barak to battle again against an army of invaders. After the battle she wrote a victory song which is part of the Book of Judges.

My ministry team member wrote this on my name tag: Debbie, a leader of new things. She then spoke over me, "Debbie, God has called you to be a leader of new things and just like Deborah in the Bible, He is calling you to lead His people in victory." Wow, that short sentence packed a punch. Not to mention the words she spoke over me. I had to take several minutes to collect myself because God started to minister to me through that sentence and her words. Suffice it to say, I now fully embrace my name and what God has called me to do.

Blessing Leadership

Scripture makes it clear we are called to pray for those in authority over us. We don't have to agree with or even like them, but we must honor and pray for them (see 1 Timothy 2:1-2; 1 Peter 2:17). Remember the Governor's prayer call from chapter 8. I shared that we don't have to agree or ask God to bless their choices and actions. Instead, we bless them to come into alignment with all God's plans and purposes. Only God knows the plans and intentions He has for an individual, so we bless them in accordance with God's intentions. We don't have to make it complicated; we just stay in blessing mode and away from cursing. I feel blessing leadership is one of the more difficult areas for us to comprehend and embrace. Because of that, I have included some examples to help.

Here are a couple blessings I often speak over my enemies, or those in authority or in governmental positions:

164

- I declare the righteousness and revelation of God be poured out upon your life. May all God's plans and purpose for your life come to pass in Jesus' name.

- May all God's plans and purposes for your life begin to bear fruit and come to fulfillment. May the Lord make Himself known to you in a real and tangible way and I decree that you will come into agreement and perfect alignment with God's plans and purposes for you.

You can take it a step further and ask God to show you prophetically what His plans and purposes are for a specific person in authority. I won't tell you by name which Governor this following blessing was written for, but suffice it to say, I and several others in our church leadership, found ourselves in a particular season of wanting to only speak curses over this individual. I knew this was wrong but as the Old Testament would say, this individual was "Doing evil in the sight of the Lord." So, I asked God to show me what He wanted us to pray as a group and how we were to bless this person instead of cursing them. This is what I felt led to pray:

> *We bless the Governor to come into the fullness and revelation of who God is and that he sees God's hand working during this virus. May the Governor recognize the hand of God is upon our State. We bless the leadership around our Governor to be Godly and full of wisdom and through it all, may our Governor come to know Jesus as Lord and Savior. Give the Governor Godly courage, knowledge, and strategy. May our state's actions and decisions flow from God's heart toward ALL His people, big and small. Amen.*

Blessings are important for everyday living and help us keep Christ at the center of our heart and mind. For this last section, I have listed some Scriptures and given sample blessings as well. I chose these specific categories because they are the more common areas we find ourselves dealing with or needing encouragement in daily.

Blessing of Victory

But no instrument forged against you will be allowed to hurt you, and no voice raised to condemn you will successfully prosecute you. It's that simple; this is how it will be for the servants of the Eternal; I will vindicate them.

Isaiah 54:17 the Voice

- God will not allow any weapon forged against me to cause me harm. God, may you vindicate and protect me so I will not be condemned or prosecuted.

But thanks be to God! He gives us the victory through our Lord Jesus Christ.

I Corinthians 15:57 NIV

- May God grant you victory because of the sacrifice of Jesus Christ.

No, in all these things we are more than conquerors through him who loved us.

Romans 8:37 NIV

- May you know that you are more than a conqueror in ALL things simply because Jesus loves you.

Blessing of Health and Fruitfulness

He himself bore our sins in his body on the tree, that we might die to sin and live to righteousness. By his wounds you have been healed.

1 Peter 2:24 ESV

- May your body manifest the truth that you have been healed!

But he was wounded for our transgressions; he was crushed for our iniquities; upon him was the chastisement that brought us peace, and with his stripes we are healed.

Isaiah 53:5 ESV

• May you receive the fullness of your healing that Christ paid the price for with His blood. May His peace flow through every area of your life.

Beloved, I pray that all may go well with you and that you may be in good health, as it goes well with your soul.

3 John 1:2 ESV

• May it go well for you and may you be in good health as your soul prospers.

For I will restore health to you, and your wounds I will heal, declares the LORD, because they have called you an outcast: 'It is Zion, for whom no one cares!'

Jeremiah 30:17 ESV

• The Lord declares He will heal your wounds and restore your health. May you receive the fullness of all He has done for you.

He is like a tree planted by streams of water that yields its fruit in its season, and its leaf does not wither. In all that he does, he prospers.

Psalm 1:3 ESV

• May your roots go deep and drink from the river of living water. As you are planted in Christ may you prosper in all that you say and do. May you bear good fruit in season.

Behold, children are a heritage from the LORD, the fruit of the womb is a reward.

Psalm 127:3 NKJV

- May your womb be fruitful, and the Lord grant you children.

Blessed is everyone who fears the LORD, who walks in His ways. When you eat the labor of your hands, you shall be happy, and it shall be well with you. Your wife shall be like a fruitful vine in the very heart of your house, your children like olive plants all around your table. Behold, thus shall the man be blessed who fears the LORD.

Psalm 128:1-4 NKJV

- Blessed are you because you fear the Lord and walk with Him. May you be filled with joy and your house ring with the sounds of laughter. May the work of your hands provide a bountiful harvest to provide for your family.

Prosperity

And God is able to bless you abundantly, so that in all things at all times, having all that you need, you will abound in every good work.

2 Corinthians 9:8 NIV

- May God abundantly bless you in all things, so you have everything you need.

You shall remember the LORD your God, for it is he who gives you power to get wealth, that he may confirm his covenant that he swore to your fathers, as it is this day.

Deuteronomy 8:18 ESV

- May you always remember and know that it is God who grants you the ability to obtain wealth. May He impart to you revelation and insight for how to walk in it.

This Book of the Law shall not depart from your mouth, but you shall meditate on it day and night, so that you may be careful to do according to all that is written in it. For then you will make your way prosperous, and then you will have good success.

Joshua 1:8 ESV

- As you meditate on God's word and obey Him, may you be prosperous and always have success.

Blessed shall you be in the city and blessed shall you be in the country. "Blessed shall be the fruit of your body, the produce of your ground and the increase of your herds, the increase of your cattle and the offspring of your flocks. "Blessed shall be your basket and your kneading bowl."

Deuteronomy 28:3-5 NKJV

- May the blessings of the Lord increase and overflow in every area of your life and every place you find yourself. May you be blessed with strong and healthy children and may the work of your hands bring constant and uninterrupted supply.

The LORD will command the blessing on you in your storehouses and in all to which you set your hand, and He will bless you in the land which the LORD your God is giving you.

Deuteronomy 28:8. NKJV

- May God command a blessing upon your finances, savings, and all you set your hand to and may He bring you to your place of promise.

For I know the plans I have for you," declares the Lord, "plans to prosper you and not to harm you, plans to give you hope and a future.

Jeremiah 29:11 NIV

- God has a future for you filled with hope and prosperity. May you know and receive it fully.

And my God will supply every need of yours according to his riches in glory in Christ Jesus.

Philippians 4:19 ESV

- May God supply every one of your needs.

Please note, the list above of subjects and companion Scriptures is by no means an exhaustive list. I encourage you to think of other categories, Scriptures, and to write more blessings.

Legacy Builders

Prayer

God help me to receive You and Your Kingdom like a child. Show me how to live a lifestyle of blessing so I may release them as a part of who I am and as an overflow of who You are in me. God, sometimes I find it difficult to pray for others who don't seem to be walking in Godly principles or wholesome character. Forgive me for neglecting my responsibility to pray for those I do not care for. Release the Holy Spirit to give me revelation and show me prophetically how and what to pray so these individuals can begin to walk in Your plans and purposes for their lives. Amen.

Reflection

Why do you think children were important to Jesus?

Have you ever been a part of a blessing ceremony?

Do you pray for your leaders and those in governmental positions? Is it hard or easy for you?

What other categories and Scriptures can be added to the list above?

Blessing in Action

Seek and ask God to show you prophetically what His plans and purposes are for a specific individual in authority. Maybe your Mayor, the Governor, your country's President. Write out a prophetic blessing based on what He shows you and begin to pray it every day for the next thirty days, at a minimum.

Chapter 16
Leaving a Legacy

A good man leaves an inheritance to his children's children ...

Proverbs 13:22 ESV

What is so important about legacy? I promised I would share the "more" regarding legacy and why it wasn't my idea for a title but God's. Legacy is much like an inheritance. Some people intertwine them and use them interchangeably. Both involve leaving something for others after you're gone. You can look *legacy* and *inheritance* up in a dictionary, but they both seem to focus on monetary gain. I found an article that describes the difference so beautifully:

> A considerable difference exists between inheritance and a legacy. Anyone can leave an inheritance, which is something you pass **TO** your family or loved ones and it also fades. A legacy is something you impart **IN** your family.[85]

Inheritance is something valuable we tangibly pass to others. While a legacy is something tangible and of value that we place in others.

A good man leaves an inheritance to his children's children.

Proverbs 13:22 ESV

Consider the difference further ... when we receive an inheritance, it means someone else paid the price or worked hard for something and we receive it for free. When we receive an inheritance in the natural, it helps us move ahead. God also intended the same thing to happen for us in the spirit. The Word of God is full of promises spoken to, over, and about the children of God. We are God's children and the promises in Scripture are for us. Simply because God loves His kids, He has given us an inheritance in the kingdom of God.

What is our spiritual inheritance and what is included with it? The Bible is full of scriptures listing our spiritual inheritance as kingdom kids, some of which include salvation (see John 3:1-21), Holy Spirit baptism (see Mark 16:15-18; Acts 1:4-8), authority (see Matthew 28:18), hearing God (see John 10:1-5), healings (see Matthew 10:1; Mark 16:15-18), setting captives free (see Isaiah 61:1; John 14:12-14), raising the dead (see John 14:12-14), miracles, signs, and wonders (see John 14:12-14), just to name a few. Isn't it exciting that God, in His infinite wisdom, planned an inheritance for us as His kids? God truly is wise and good.[86]

> ... the promised Holy Spirit, who is a deposit guaranteeing our inheritance until the redemption of those who are God's possession—to the praise of his glory.
>
> Ephesians 1:13b-14 NIV

However, if we look at the difference between inheritance and legacy, where inheritance is something passing *to* us, and legacy is imparting something *within* us, we then see God went one step further. He didn't just give us an inheritance; He imparted a legacy to us. The legacy and life Jesus lived is not just His inheritance freely given to us but also the legacy of the Holy Spirit imparted to live within us.

Billy Graham once said: "The greatest legacy one can pass on to one's children and grandchildren are not money or other material things accumulated in one's life, but rather a legacy of character and faith."[87]

Just as God left us a legacy in His son Jesus, Jesus left us an even greater legacy. He paid the ultimate price of death to take on a debt none of us could bear and He did even more. Jesus showed us how to live our lives. The Gospels are Jesus' legacy of a life lived out in total devotion to His

Heavenly Father. Jesus modeled how we are to live in the earthly realm until our Heavenly Kingdom is prepared and ready for us (see John 14:3). Jesus exhibited every character trait and walked through many trials and tribulations in His life. He did this all to show us the many facets of the Father's love and how to live a life pleasing to Him.

He didn't stop there. Jesus not only blessed children (see Mark 10:13-16; Like 18:15-17), He blessed His followers, the people listening, His disciples (see Matthew 5:3-12; Luke 6:20-22) and of course, He even blessed the bread when He broke it (see Matthew 26:26-28; Mark 14:22–24; Luke 22:19–20; 1 Corinthians 11:23–25). On His day of ascension (see Luke 24:50-52). He blessed and commissioned His disciples and the new emerging church. He told them He was leaving but He was sending and giving us a legacy in the form of the Holy Spirit.

The year before I launched my ministry, I went through the pastoral licensing course for our denomination. In one of the final papers I wrote for class, I discussed the topic of inheritance. The instructor asked me if I would prepare a mini-sermon and share on the concept of inheritance with the class. He told me to think of it as a speech a valedictorian might share with their graduating class. I was honored he saw me this way and valued what I had to say on the topic. However, I never gave much thought to the word *legacy* or the difference between a legacy and an inheritance until 2020 when our family began to pray regarding what we believed God was asking us to do.

We had been working with a financial advisor for many months to begin getting things "in order" for the time John would eventually retire from his corporate software engineering job. At that time, we still had at least fifteen years before he would "officially" be eligible to retire at age sixty-five. We were also senior pastoring full time, and should the church grow, or God ask us to focus all our time and energy on serving Him, we wanted to be financially able to do so. Then everything changed. Looking back, I can see now that God was positioning us to make a significant life transition and change. He was setting us up to be able to respond when He spoke. God was about to speak a "suddenly" to us.

In October/November of 2020, God told us He wanted to move us to South Carolina. Not in fifteen years when we retired, but sooner and that we had better get moving and take steps. We asked our immediate family to pray with us and we discussed it at Thanksgiving. Our kids and my mother said they had heard God too and were coming with us. When I prayed about the move, I asked God why South Carolina and why now. His response was so that we could leave a legacy for our family and our community and help others build legacies in their families. Many thought we would start another church, but God had other plans. He had begun talking to the family about becoming entrepreneurs and starting a small business. We had no idea what business venture at the time but that whole adventure is still in process and a story for another book. Legacy is always important to God but there is something extra special in this current season God wants to impart to His people.

The Rest of the Story

If you recall, I promised to share the rest of my mother's story and how she crafts and writes blessings based on Scripture. My mother is a student of the Word. She reads, studies, and spends time in prayer. She is also a powerful intercessor and seer. A seer is someone who operates in the prophetic, but their main avenue of communication with God is through seeing in the spiritual realm. When she and her friend began blessing one another weekly, they started with the first fruit of the spirit: love. She completed an entire year of weekly blessings on love. My mother's friend was more spontaneous with her blessings. She would find a Scripture, read the Scripture, and then flow freely with spiritual encouragement, speaking over my mother and blessing her spirit.

On the other hand, my mother would choose a verse, read the verse, the commentary, and anything else she could find regarding the deeper meaning of the verse. She would then take her notes and pray over them as she began crafting a written blessing. The blessing would then encompass all she had learned about that specific verse.

Once the blessing was written out, my mom would then call each person on her list and leave a voice message reading the written blessing. Sometimes she would free flow at the end and add what the Spirit was speaking. We all knew not to answer our phones on Wednesday morning when we saw her name on the caller ID, so she could speak the blessing and it would be recorded on our voicemail to save. By the time my mom had to stop, to focus on caring for my ailing father, she was calling over fifteen people weekly and speaking blessings over them. I was one of those people. In fact, if you were to look at my voice mailbox on my phone, I still have over forty messages saved. The rest I have forward to my email and stored on my computer. The blessings are powerful and life-giving. When I need encouragement, I go back and listen to them.

When I released my book with Chosen in 2018, I offered special gifts to my launch team members and some to those who preordered the book to help boost sales. One of the items, as part of the extra gifts, were my mom's blessings. She took two primary Scriptures I used in *The Gift of Prophetic Encouragement* book and crafted blessings. My daughter created a beautiful printable of the blessings that could be framed, and she also recorded them as an mp3 file for easy listening. This was one of my favorite *"freebies"* because I love blessings so much and it paired so well with the topic of prophetic encouragement. If you want, you can still access the free printable blessings. I have included them on my website[88] under the freebies tab; there are four different choices. What better way to speak a blessing than to use Scripture as the foundation!

This is just one example of my mom, Connie McEldowney's, blessings. As you read the blessing below, I know you will be encouraged, blessed, and filled with life.

> *Beloved, I call your spirit to attention. Listen as I read God's word from Hebrews 3:13.*
>
> *But encourage one another daily, as long as it is called Today, so that none of you may be hardened by sin's deceitfulness.*
>
> *God wants us to stay in fellowship with other believers. As we talk to one another about our mutual faith, we will become aware of the deceitfulness that attracts us and tries to destroy us. He wants us to encourage one another with love and concern.*
>
> *Spirit, I bless you to daily speak words of encouragement to one another. I bless you to be steadfast and full of confidence as you step out in faith and provide assurance to those around*

you. This encouragement will build an underlying foundation of things hoped for. I bless you to remain steadfast until the hope is realized. This is the time to encourage one another and to never be stubborn or hardened by sin's deceitfulness. I bless you spirit to know that even the strongest of God's people need the help of other Christians. Sin has so many ways and colors that we need more eyes than our own.

I bless your faith to grow and to be stirred to a life of obedient faith as you come along side one another daily to speak words of encouragement so that those who listen will hear God's voice and respond in love and obedience.

I bless you in the name of Jesus of Nazareth.

WOW! Powerful, isn't it? I know that it may take some time for individuals to build up to crafting and writing blessings that are more than a sentence or two. However, it's a skill we can learn and work towards. Every individual my mother called each week was blessed. I know as she pronounced these blessings over us, she was doing so **by faith.** There was no doubt in her mind God would indeed back the blessings because, after all, He inspired[89] and initiated all Scripture.

> *By faith Isaac blessed Jacob and Esau concerning things to come.*
> *By faith Jacob, when he was dying, blessed both the sons of Joseph; and worshipped, leaning upon the top of his staff.*
> Hebrews 11:20-21 NKJV

There is no doubt in my mind my mother will be commended for her faith when she stands before the throne at the end of her life. This is one legacy my mother has imparted to all who received her blessings. And this is a legacy we, too, can impart.

The Importance of Legacy

God is a God of legacy. We see this in the way He interacted with Adam and Eve, Abraham, Jacob, Moses, Joshua, Gideon, David, and others. God loves us and longs to have a relationship with us on a long-term basis. He is in it to win with us by His side.

> *Now it is God who makes both us and you stand firm in Christ. He anointed us, set his seal of ownership on us, and put his Spirit in our hearts as a deposit, guaranteeing what is to come.*
> 2 Corinthians 1:21-22 NIV

God not only anoints us, but He sets His seal of ownership on us. He puts His Spirit in our hearts as a "deposit" guaranteeing what He has for us. God is the one who anoints us. It's this anointing from the Lord which sets us apart and empowers us to function in the supernatural gifts of the Holy Spirit. We are His legacy here on the earth. We need the anointing of the Lord to prepare us for the work ahead and to fulfill our mandate here on the earth.

Legacy Builders

Prayer

Father God, I acknowledge you are a good, good Father and You have left a rich inheritance for me as Your child. Thank you for anointing me and setting Your seal of ownership upon me. Thank you for the gift of Your son Jesus and the gift of the Holy Spirit. They left a powerful legacy for me to follow. Lord, help me to be a living legacy for You all the days of my life upon the earth. Show me the plans and work You have prepared for me and help me to fulfill every last one of them. Amen.

Reflection

How do you view the difference between inheritance and legacy?

What legacy has God imparted to you and your family?

What kind of legacy do you want to leave for others?

Blessing in Action

Ask God for the name of someone at your church you don't know very well. Write out and give them a prophetic word of encouragement.

Chapter 17
Crafting a Blessing

... And a voice from heaven said, "This is my
Son, whom I love; with him I am well pleased."
Matthew 3:17 NIV

The time had finally come for me to teach my first class on blessings. I had fulfilled all of Papa Carl's requirements and answered all his questions satisfactorily. I was excited and so were Papa Carl and his wife, Donna. Even though Papa Carl questioned me along the way and pushed me hard to consider many aspects of the blessings, I wasn't prepared for one thing.

Sitting on the front row of class that night was a man I'll call Ron. It was so many years ago I can't remember his real name, but his actions and words made a lasting impression on me and taught me a valuable lesson. The further I got into my teaching the more upset Ron seemed to get. I felt this way because he started out sitting normally, leaning in as he listened to the teaching. As I neared the end of the teaching; however, his body language had changed, and he seemed disgruntled. He crossed his arms across his chest and then began to sit up straighter, taller, and seemed rigged if that was even possible.

As soon as my teaching was finished, I had the class break into ministry groups to work on blessings. Ron immediately came to talk with me. I could tell he was still upset because he still had his arms crossed. He was tall and somewhat oversized but not overweight. He reminded me of a football player on the front line of defense. I greeted him and asked if everything was ok. "No, not really," was his reply.

"Oh," I responded, "was the teaching not Biblical enough? Or maybe you wonder if it's still for today?"

He laughed, "No, you covered those points pretty well, so I have no doubt blessings are Biblical and for today."

I wondered aloud just what was it that had him so upset. I searched my brain for every possible scenario that could present a problem, but I was coming up blank. I just looked at him, waiting for him to respond.

"Well, Debbie, I get the idea and concept of blessings, but I can't do what you are asking me to do. I can't and I won't," he stated emphatically.

"Uhh, ok," I stammered before collecting my thoughts. "What exactly is it you can't do?"

"I cannot speak blessings about God kissing people and how lovely they are like flowers after the rain. I just don't speak like that, and I can't do it!"

Inside I breathed a sigh of relief and was laughing. On the outside, I did my best to stay composed. "Ok, so you don't have an issue with the concept of speaking blessings but it's the mechanics of what to say that's the problem?"

"YES! Exactly. I'm not the kind of guy that says touchy-feely things, so now what do I do?" he asked.

One of the examples I gave was from Janice Seney's email signature: "May the Goodness of God chase you down and tackle you. May his Mercy hold you in place as His Grace Kisses your life."

I started laughing and replied, "All right, so what do you like? Sports? Fishing? Cars?"

His eyes lit up, "Football! I love football."

Great, I thought to myself, *the one sport I knew nothing about except the Superbowl has excellent commercials*. I thought for a moment, took a deep breath, and said, "Terrific, then this week, see if you can come up with just ONE blessing based on football. Do you think you can do that?"

"I'll try," he replied, then walked away to join his ministry group.

The following week Ron hurriedly searched me out. "Debbie, I got it. You won't believe it, but I did exactly what you asked."

Honestly, I had forgotten all about the assignment I had given him until he rushed to the front of the classroom, waving his notebook around. "All right, Ron, let's hear what you've got."

He was so excited you would have thought he was a kid in a candy store. He opened his notebook and proceeded to read his blessing based on football.

"'May you receive all God is passing your way today!' Do you get it? In Football, they pass the ball."

"Yes, Ron, I get it." I laughed. "I might not know much about football, but I do know they pass the ball. That's great and I am so glad you could come up with one blessing based on football."

"Oh no, Debbie. I came up with way more than one blessing. Do you want to hear more?"

Of course, I did. For the next several minutes, Ron read through the blessings he had written based on different aspects of football. I was delighted. Ron was excited. He now had blessings he would be comfortable speaking over people. God is so good and faithful.

You may not like football as Ron did or feel like you can't speak a flowery, gushy blessing similar the one I shared above, though I firmly believe you can, if you try. I suggest coming up with blessings you will look forward to speaking over someone else.

Many years after my experience with Ron, I had another fun encounter with a student following class. I had just finished teaching on blessings when a young man named Keith Rabe approached me and laughing said, "Blessings are God's pick me up lines!" I hadn't thought about it that way, but YES. Blessings are like a pick up line. God wants to pick us up and add more people to His family. The whole point of spreading the good news of the Gospel is to introduce people to a real, loving, good God who loves with an everlasting, unconditional love. Blessings can be a fun way to introduce someone to the love and joy of Jesus in a non-threatening creative way.

Samples of Blessings

If you work in a place where you must be careful about saying the name of God, you can still speak and pronounce blessings. God knows your heart as you speak and pronounce blessings over others, and He will still *target* them for good. Below are some samples of what a blessing may look like, then a version of the same blessing with the "Christian speak" removed.

> May you be surprised by the goodness of God today.
> May you be surprised by all the good coming your way today.

> May you be refreshed in the Lord like a flower after a spring rain.
> May you be refreshed today like a flower after the spring rain.

> May God joyfully carry you toward the goal line as you forge ahead through opposition.
> As you press forward through opposition, may you reach the goal line with joy.

In the next chapter, I'll give more examples and share even more blessing activation exercises. I know if the body of Christ can capture the intent and heart of the Father to speak and release blessings to others, we will see lives changed. Spoken blessings have the potential to be good "word bombs" that can have ongoing Holy Spirit explosions of joy and encouragement. God loves people and wants to target them for good, but He needs cooperation to partner with Him to speak blessings, allowing him to intentionally target others for good. Are you ready to accept the challenge? Will you Dare2Hear from heaven to release His intended blessings to others?

Earlier in chapter 12, "How and Who We Bless," we learned the different elements a verbal blessing has. They were: Our words, God's Word, and God's name. I also mentioned that blessings can be proclamations made privately or publicly. I am a firm believer there is power when they are spoken. I know it may seem scary to some but there is power and authority when we speak. Sometimes it may not be possible to speak the blessing, in which case you can write it out and impart it that way. However, with today's technology, we can do so much more with the written blessing in speaking it. We can send a text or record a video or voice message to send and there are other ways to impart blessings.

Ways to give Blessings

- Speaking directly to the person—face to face.
- Send voice or video recorded messages.
- Write and send a blessing in a:
  ° Letter
  ° Email
  ° Card
  ° Note (for example: you can leave a message for a waitress on the receipt or leave a note on someone's car)
  ° Call and speak a blessing over the phone

We all need to memorize and remember the verse found in Ephesians 4:29:

> Let no unwholesome word proceed from your mouth, but only such a word as is good for edification according to the need of the moment, so that it will give grace to those who hear. (NASB)

We are charged with the task of not just keeping our own mouth from speaking "unwholesome" words, but we are to speak edification and encouragement in the moment. What moment? Any conversation, interaction, or moment we find ourselves in is an opportunity to speak a blessing.

Legacy Builders

Prayer

Father, help me to be creative in thinking outside the box as I look for ways to be not only be a blessing but to speak blessings to others. As I speak life to others, continually pour out Your grace upon me so they can receive Your grace as well. Amen

Reflection

When was the last time you sent or received a letter via regular mail?

Think of a hobby or something you like to do. How many blessings can you write around these topics?

If God was going to speak a "pick up" line to you, what might it be?

Write a blessing like the samples above—one using God's name and one with the same sentiment without His name.

Blessing in Action

Ask God to give you the name of a person you don't see regularly. Write an old-fashioned letter to them and include a future prophetic blessing in it.

Chapter 18
Exercises in Blessing

*By faith Isaac blessed Jacob and Esau concerning
things to come.*

Hebrews 11:20 NKJV

This chapter is designed to walk you through the process of crafting
blessings. If you were in a class and I were teaching face-to-face, we would
spend a great deal of time working through the mechanics of how to write
a blessing, whom to write them for, and sharing them with one another so
we could then "grow" our library of blessings. I would give time during
class for you to work on crafting some simple, basic activations and then
assign you homework. Your homework would be to deliver one of the
blessings you wrote to someone in your family, a friend, at church, or an
individual you come across as you are out and about in the marketplace.

Are you ready to write your own blessings? I will include several
examples and then also give you a creative list you can use to begin to
craft a blessing. I will provide you with a list of Scriptures from which
you can write blessings but know the Bible is full of many more than I
list. Then I will ask you to kick it up a notch and write future prophetic
blessings.

God's Pick Me Up Lines

General Blessings:

May the kindness of God surprise you today when it jumps right out in front of you.

May the great goodness of God hug you as His grace and mercy kiss your life.

May the peace of God flood your heart and mind today.

May God strengthen you for the work week ahead.

Blessings From an Item:

Coffee ~ May you get an extra jolt of energy today.
Pumpkin Spice Latte ~ May you experience the sweetness of God today.
Rain ~ As the rain revives the land, may God revive you. **OR**
As the rain revives the land, may you too be revived.
Rain ~ May the dry areas of your life become green and lush like the grass after a spring rain.
Football ~ I declare the goals you have set in your life shall bring you victory!
Clock ~ God is not finished with you yet. He still has time to bring His promises to pass.
Time ~ Time is not running out for you. Many areas of your life are just beginning.

Blessings From Grocery Store Items:

Close-Up Toothpaste ~ May you experience God close up!

Skittles: The rainbow of colors ~ May you receive all the promises God has for you.

Peanut Butter Cups: Two great tastes that go great together ~ you and God are great together, just like peanut butter and chocolate.

Legacy Builder Exercise

Write Blessings Based on these items:

Skittles	Milky Way	Light	Laughter
Coffee	Tea	Friendship	Oasis
Football	Baseball	Salt	Ocean
Tulips	Roses	Keys	Mountains
Sunshine	Rain	Kite	River
Clock	Time	Gift	Oak Tree

Write Blessings Based on these Biblical Words:

Love	Joy	Hope	Rejoice
Peace	Patience	Glory	New
Kindness	Goodness	Favor	Freedom
Faithfulness	Gentleness	Grace	Accepted
Forgiveness	Self-control	Victory	Beauty
Breakthrough	Mercy	Miracle	Restoration

Write Blessings Based on these Scriptures

Deuteronomy 28:8	Joshua 1:9
Jeremiah 29:11	Jeremiah 31:3
Psalms 1:3	Psalms 21:5-7
Proverbs 23:24	Hebrews 3:13
Ephesians 1:3-4	Philippians 4:19
1 Corinthians 14:1	3 John 1:2

Write Blessings Based on the Names of God

For this exercise, write a blessing based on the names of God. Here are a few of His names to get you started:

- **Jehovah Jireh:** The LORD our provider (Genesis 22:14)
- **Jehovah Rapha:** The LORD our Healer (Exodus 15:26)
- **Jehovah Nissi:** The LORD our Banner (Exodus 17:15)
- **Jehovah Shalom:** The LORD our Peace (Judges 6:24)
- **Jehovah Raah:** The LORD our Shepherd (Psalms 23:1)
- **Jehovah Tsidkenu:** The LORD our Righteousness (Jeremiah 23:6)
- **Jehovah Shammah:** The LORD is Here (Ezekiel 48:35)
- **Jehovah Sabaoth**: The Lord of Hosts (1 Samuel 1:3, 11)

Write Your Own Blessings

For this portion, I want you to ask the Lord for a specific person to write a blessing for. Spend time in worship and prayer, seeking God's heart for this individual. Write down the word, thoughts, impressions, pictures, and Scriptures that come to mind. Then craft a future-looking prophetic blessing for them. Remember, a future-looking prophetic blessing will speak to the potential of what someone can or will do later. Once it is done, set aside a time to speak it over them. I also suggest giving them a written copy.

Blessings in Action

Extra Legacy Builder Exercises:

1. Speak a good word to a coworker or friend today.
2. Speak a blessing over each family member in the next twenty-four hours. Write down what you say. Then repeat that blessing in writing within a week.
3. Speak an encouraging word to a salesperson today.
4. Speak a blessing over the grocery store clerk today.
5. Look around you. Do you see someone with special potential? Tell the person what *gold* you see. (Write about your experience)
6. Ask God to give you a blessing for a leader in your church today. Then be sure to bless them.
7. Ask God to give you the name of a person you can bless today. Then be sure to bless that person.
8. Speak a blessing over someone you don't know as you go about your life today.

Legacy Builders

Prayer

God, I am eager and ready to start blessing others. As I step out and begin to implement all I have learned in reading this book, release Your Holy Spirit to help guide me. Holy Spirit open my ears, eyes, and heart to be attentive to You. Allow me to know your heart for others. I want to be a gift to others and affect the atmosphere around me. Allow me to be Your agent of blessings and release arrows of the Holy Spirit to touch and move the hearts of those You ask me to bless. Amen.

Reflection

Can you see how God uses blessings as "Pick me up lines"?

Can you recall a time when God spoke a "pick me up line" to you? What was it and how did it make you feel?

How do you hope the blessings above will impact those you give them to?

Blessing in Action

As you work your way through this chapter, work on writing your own blessings, and specifically ask God who each one is for. Then make sure to write it out, give them a copy, speak it over them, and bless them.

Be sure to work your way through each of the extra activations in the *Blessings in Action* section above and continually repeat them to ensure they become a part of your daily life.

Chapter 19
Be A Blessing

*Train up a child in the way he should go; even
when he is old, he will not depart from it.*
                                         Proverbs 22:6 ESV

Throughout this book, we've talked a lot about what it means to bless others, what a blessing is, and how we can be a blessing. We are called to do more than love, show kindness, extend a smile, and give a helping hand. We are called to be a blessing. The legacy we leave behind and impart to others is not just in learning this lost art. It is much more than that. First, we must learn how to bless and then begin to bless. Next, we must teach and equip others to bless as well. As we read Scripture, we can see they were not just a valuable commodity, but a central part of the Jewish life and they should be in the life of the believer today. The act of blessing others may have been a lost art for a period, but we can change that. Not all is lost, we can redeem and reinstate their value of blessing today and in the process, we will become a blessing.

There is one blessing I have yet to mention and that is the Blessing of Abraham in Genesis 12. I intentionally saved it for last because there is a key element we must also understand. Blessings are not just for others; they are for us as well.

*"I will make you into a great nation,
and I will bless you;
I will make your name great,*

*and **you will be a blessing**.*
I will bless those who bless you,
and whoever curses you I will curse;
and all peoples on earth
will be blessed through you."
Genesis 12:2-3 NIV

We are not just to receive blessings, but we are to *BE A BLESSING* to others. In these verses, God is pronouncing a future prophetic blessing over Abraham and all the people of the earth. God intends for us to receive the blessing and become *the* blessing. The life we live as Christ followers is to be a blessing to others.

Many prosperity gospel preachers have twisted this and other scriptures to emphasize their "name it and claim it" theology. However, if we shy away from discussing passages of Scriptures because others have abused them, we are missing key elements and instructions containing God's intended blessings.

God is much more concerned that we prosper in *all* areas of our lives, not just financially. The world's answer to solving all our problems is financial prosperity. However, we know the natural world often contradicts God's kingdom. Earthly prosperity is not kingdom prosperity.

> *For what will it profit a man if he gains the whole*
> *world [wealth, fame, success], but forfeits his soul?*
> *Or what will a man give in exchange for his soul?*
> Matthew 16:26 AMP

I would say that financial prosperity isn't as important to God as our soul and spiritual prosperity are to Him. God wants us to have blessings overflowing in every area of our life.

> *All praise to God, the Father of our Lord Jesus*
> *Christ, who has blessed us with every spiritual*
> *blessing in the heavenly realms because we are*
> *united with Christ.*
> Ephesians 1:3 NLT

God wants us to live in His SOZO prosperity. Sozo is a Greek word found in the New Testament 110 times.

Sozo Definition[90]

1. to save, keep safe and sound, to rescue from danger or destruction
   a. one (from injury or peril)
      1. to save a suffering one (from perishing), i.e., one suffering from disease, to make well, heal, restore to health
      2. to preserve one who is in danger of destruction, to save or rescue
   b. to save in the technical biblical sense
      1. negatively
   c. to deliver from the penalties of the Messianic judgment
   d. to save from the evils which obstruct the reception of the Messianic deliverance

Sozo means to be: Saved, whole, healed, delivered, preserved, and well in our body, soul, and spirit.

> *Beloved, I pray that in every way you may prosper and enjoy good health, as your soul prospers.*
> 3 John 1:2 Berean Study Bible

We are called to prosper in every area of life just as our soul prospers. However, many individuals today are not flourishing, nor are their souls. They may have financial prosperity, but their soul is sick. Many people struggle with fear, loneliness, isolation, depression, hopelessness, regret, and more. These soul issues can only be solved as we accept the whole experience of the Sozo of God.

> People whose spirit needs to be called to life and enlarged cannot meet God deeply, if at all. They cannot embrace life or themselves fully, and they cannot connect with the spirit and heart of another person.
> ~ Sylvia Gunter[91]

Be the Gift

You and I are a gift. Even if we may not yet see ourselves as such, God sees the potential He has placed within each of us. He invites us to partner with Him to extend His love and blessings to a dying and lonely world.

> *If you fully obey the LORD your God and carefully follow all his commands I give you today, the LORD your God will set you high above all the nations on earth. All these blessings will come on you and accompany you if you obey the LORD your God.*
>
> Deuteronomy 28:1-2 NIV)

God continues for another ten verses in Deuteronomy 28 after His opening statements. He is charging those who love Him not to just follow Him but to follow (obey) His commands carefully. Not just a select few but all the instructions He has outlined throughout His Word. We are commanded to love, bless, encourage, speak the truth, and so much more.

We can show the love of Jesus and bless others through our actions, but it is also important to do this through our words. Our words have authority and power and when we attach the name of God to our blessings, He will not only bless others through us but we are blessed in return.

If you recall, from chapter 1 in the Torah, blessings are seen as a conduit for spiritual and physical potential. When we become a blessing, we are a conduit for the Holy Spirit to work in and through us, to bless the lives of others so they may reach their full spiritual and physical potential. God needs us to be a blessing and awaken others to this powerful truth.

> *"God our Father is rousing our spirit and waking the dead places in us. We are being called to awaken the slumbering spirits of others."* ~ Sylvia Gunter[92]

Don't forget that everything we have, and all that we are, comes from God and God alone. We love because He first loved us. We bless because He first blessed us. God is our source for every good and perfect gift we call blessings.

Praise be to the God and Father of our Lord Jesus Christ, who has blessed us in the heavenly realms with every spiritual blessing in Christ. For he chose us in him before the creation of the world to be holy and blameless in his sight...

Ephesians 1:3-4 NIV

We live in a negative, dying world where many have lost hope and have nowhere to turn. They are wandering around lost, waiting for someone to reveal the truth and point them toward life. Jesus is the answer to all we face in this world. It's too good a truth to keep to ourselves. So, I end this book the way I started it: I want to issue you a challenge. I want to dare you to resurrect in your own life the lost art of blessing others. Become a legacy. Impart the legacy of Jesus Christ to others and open them up to the truth He has revealed to you. Begin to speak and release blessings to others. In the process, I promise you will also become a blessing.

Dedicate your children to God and point them in the way that they should go, and the values they've learned from you will be with them for life.

Proverbs 22:6 TPT

We are God's children. He has marked us, chosen us, and dedicated us to Himself. Throughout the Word, he has shown us the values and lessons we need to live with in this life. His Word has been given to equip and train us in the way we should go. Now let us return to them.

But you are not like that, for you are a chosen people. You are royal priests, a holy nation, God's very own possession. As a result, you can show others the goodness of God, for he called you out of the darkness into his wonderful light.

1 Peter 2:9 NLT

God chose us. He gave Jesus to us as an inheritance and a legacy. Those who follow Christ, and His Word are His legacy to the world.

But you are God's chosen treasure—priests who are kings, a spiritual "nation" set apart as God's devoted ones. He called you out of darkness to experience his marvelous light, and now he claims you as his very own. He did this so that you would broadcast his glorious wonders throughout the world.

1 Peter 2:9 TPT

Endnotes

1 https://www.myjewishlearning.com/article/blessings-a-conduit-of-infinite-potential/
2 https://www.chabad.org/library/article_cdo/aid/987904/jewish/How-Many-Blessings-does-a-Jew-Say-Each-Day.htm and https://aish.com/43-100-blessings-each-day/
3 https://www.myjewishlearning.com/article/blessings-a-conduit-of-infinite-potential/
4 https://www.myjewishlearning.com/article/blessings-a-conduit-of-infinite-potential/
5 https://faithgateway.com/blogs/christian-books/the-promise-of-blessing/
6 Kerry Kirkwood, The Power of Blessing, (Shippensburg, PA, Destiny Image, 2010) page 19-20
7 Debbie Kitterman, Releasing God's Heart: Through Hearing His Voice, (Dare2Hear Ministries, Sound the Call Publications, 2008, revised 2011) page 65.
8 Peter M. Lord, Bless and Be Blessed, How Your Word Can Make a Difference, (Grand Rapids, Michigan, Revell, 2004), page 36.
9 https://www.psychologytoday.com/us/blog/the-right-mindset/202010/10-ways-apply-the-3-1-positivity-ratio 2020
10 https://educationandbehavior.com/how-to-help-students-with-behavior-problems/ 2021
11 https://www.todayschristianwoman.com/articles/2008/september/7.26.html 2008 article
12 https://www.todayschristianwoman.com/articles/2008/september/7.26.html 2008 article
13 Bill Gothard, The Power of the Spoken Blessings, (Institute in Basic Life Principles 2004, Multnomah/Random House, 2008) back cover text.
14 https://braininjurysvcs.org/choose-wisely-how-our-words-impact-others/
15 Debbie Kitterman, Releasing God's Heart: Through Hearing His Voice, (Dare2Hear Ministries, Sound the Call Publications, 2008, revised 2011), page 59.
16 https://braininjurysvcs.org/choose-wisely-how-our-words-impact-others/
17 https://www.thoughtco.com/how-much-of-your-body-is-water-609406
18 https://www.draikoofficial.com/
19 https://biblehealing.wordpress.com/who-is-dr-aiko-hormann-whats-her-role-in-sozo/
20 Catherine Thorpe, Healing Timeline: https://www.amazon.com/Healing-Timeline-Shalom-Present-Future/dp/0981913709
21 Debbie Kitterman, Releasing God's Heart: Through Hearing His Voice, (Dare2Hear Ministries, Sound the Call Publications, 2008, revised 2011) page 57.
22 https://www.biblestudytools.com/lexicons/hebrew/kjv/barak.html
23 https://www.bibletools.org/index.cfm/fuseaction/Lexicon.show/ID/G2127/eulogeo.html
24 Baker's Evangelical Dictionary of Theology https://www.biblestudytools.com/dictionary/blessing/
25 Baker's Evangelical Dictionary of Theology https://www.biblestudytools.com/dictionary/blessing/
26 Baker's Evangelical Dictionary of Theology https://www.biblestudytools.com/dictionary/blessing/
27 https://www.dictionary.com/browse/eulogy

28 https://www.merriam-webster.com/dictionary/eulogy

29 https://www.merriam-webster.com/dictionary/eulogy

30 https://www.betterplaceforests.com/blog/articles/how-to-write-a-eulogy-for-your-loved-one

31 Peter M. Lord, Bless and Be Blessed, How Your Word Can Make a Difference, (Grand Rapids, Michigan, Revell, 2004), page 48.

32 https://www.biblestudytools.com/dictionary/covenant/

33 https://www.dictionary.com/browse/blessing

34 https://www.dictionary.com/browse/promise

35 https://av1611.com/kjbp/kjv-dictionary/promise.html

36 https://www.biblestudytools.com/dictionary/covenant/

37 https://wikidiff.com/promise/blessing

38 https://wikidiff.com/promise/covenant

39 https://www.biblestudytools.com/dictionary/covenant/

40 https://www.biblestudytools.com/dictionary/covenant/

41 https://www.blueletterbible.org/lexicon/h2603/kjv/wlc/0-1/

42 https://www.blueletterbible.org/lexicon/h7965/kjv/wlc/0-1/

43 https://www.blueletterbible.org/lexicon/h7965/kjv/wlc/0-1/

44 https://rcoa.ca/shalom-the-peace-that-passes-understanding

45 https://www.blueletterbible.org/lexicon/h8034/kjv/wlc/0-1/

46 https://www.stevethomason.net/2021/08/23/the-blessing-in-numbers-622-27/

47 Kerry Kirkwood, The Power of Blessing, (Shippensburg, PA, Destiny Image, 2010) page 57.

48 Kerry Kirkwood, The Power of Blessing, (Shippensburg, PA, Destiny Image, 2010) page 57-58.

49 Kerry Kirkwood, The Power of Blessing, (Shippensburg, PA, Destiny Image, 2010) page 58.

50 https://www.physicsclassroom.com/class/newtlaws/Lesson-4/Newton-s-Third-Law

51 https://www1.grc.nasa.gov/beginners-guide-to-aeronautics/newtons-laws-of-motion

52 Bruce Wilkerson, The Prayer of Jabez: Breaking through to the Blessed Life, (Sisters, Oregon, Multnomah Publishers, 2000), page 20.

53 https://www.encyclopedia.com/arts/educational-magazines/psalm-23

54 https://www.surpassingglory.org/about-us/

55 High priest in Hebrew is Kohen

56 Dictionary.com

57 https://charismamag.com/spriritled-living/supernaturaldreams/the-access-points-you-need-for-entry-into-heavenly-portals/ from 2/3/2022

58 Peter M. Lord, Bless and Be Blessed, How Your Word Can Make a Difference, (Grand Rapids, Michigan, Revell, 2004), page 34.

59 Peter M. Lord, Bless and Be Blessed, How Your Word Can Make a Difference, (Grand Rapids, Michigan, Revell, 2004), page 33-34

60 Bill Gothard, The Power of the Spoken Blessings, (Institute in Basic Life Principles 2004, Multnomah/Random House, 2008) back cover text.

61 Peter M. Lord, Bless and Be Blessed, How Your Word Can Make a Difference, (Grand Rapids, Michigan, Revell, 2004), page 63-64.

62 Peter M. Lord, Bless and Be Blessed, How Your Word Can Make a Difference, (Grand Rapids, Michigan, Revell, 2004), page 63-64

63 Watchman Nee, Release of the Spirit, (Indianapolis, Sure Foundation)

64 Sylvia Gunter and Arthur Burke, Blessing Your Spirit, (Birmingham, AL, The Father's

Business, 2005) page v.

65 Debbie Kitterman, Releasing God's Heart: Through Hearing His Voice, (Dare2Hear Ministries, Sound the Call Publications, 2008, revised 2011), page 45.

66 Peter M. Lord, Bless and Be Blessed, How Your Word Can Make a Difference, (Grand Rapids, Michigan, Revell, 2004), page 74.8

67 https://uh.edu/~dsocs3/wisdom/wisdom/we_remember.pdf

68 https://www.td.org/insights/debunk-this-people-remember-10-percent-of-what-they-read

69 https://www.worklearning.com/2006/05/01/people_remember/

70 Peter M Lord, Bless and Be Blessed, How Your Word Can Make a Difference, (Grand Rapids, Michigan, Revell, 2004), page 27.

71 Peter M. Lord, Bless and Be Blessed, How Your Word Can Make a Difference, (Grand Rapids, Michigan, Revell, 2004), page 36.

72 Debbie Kitterman, Releasing God's Heart: Through Hearing His Voice, (Dare2Hear Ministries, Sound the Call Publications, 2008, revised 2011) page 68.

73 Debbie Kitterman, Releasing God's Heart: Through Hearing His Voice, (Dare2Hear Ministries, Sound the Call Publications, 2008, revised 2011) page 68.

74 Debbie Kitterman, The Gift of Prophetic Encouragement: Hearing the Words of God for Others, (Bloomington, MN, Chosen Books, 2018) page 19.

75 Debbie Kitterman, The Gift of Prophetic Encouragement: Hearing the Words of God for Others, (Bloomington, MN, Chosen Books, 2018), page 20.

76 https://www.myjewishlearning.com/article/blessings-a-conduit-of-infinite-potential/

77 100 Blessings, March 1, 2020 https://100blessings.org/

78 William T. Ligon, Sr., Imparting the Blessing to Your Children: What the Jewish Patriarchs Knew, (Brunswick, GA, The Fathers Blessing, 1989) page 16.

79 William T. Ligon, Sr., Imparting the Blessing to Your Children: What the Jewish Patriarchs Knew, (Brunswick, GA, The Fathers Blessing, 1989) page 1.

80 https://18doors.org/the_seven_blessings/

81 https://www.vocabulary.com/dictionary/transliteration; Unlike a translation, which tells you the meaning of a word that's written in another language, a transliteration only gives you an idea of how the word is pronounced, by putting it in a familiar alphabet.

82 https://18doors.org/the_seven_blessings/

83 https://18doors.org/the_seven_blessings/

84 Dorthy Astoria, The Name Book, (Minneapolis, Minnesota, Bethany House Publishers, 1982, 1997), page 86.

85 https://www.linkedin.com/pulse/what-difference-between-inheritance-legacy-mike-cowart/

86 Debbie Kitterman, Releasing God's Heart: Through Hearing His Voice, (Dare2Hear Ministries, Sound the Call Publications, 2008, revised 2011) page 22.

87 https://www.linkedin.com/pulse/what-difference-between-inheritance-legacy-mike-cowart/

88 https://debbiekitterman.com/freebies/

89 2 Timothy 3:16-17

90 https://www.biblestudytools.com/lexicons/greek/nas/sozo.html, Strong's 4982

91 Sylvia Gunter and Arthur Burke, Blessing Your Spirit, (Birmingham, AL, The Father's Business, 2005) page x.

92 Sylvia Gunter and Arthur Burke, Blessing Your Spirit, (Birmingham, AL, The Father's Business, 2005) page x.

Debbie is an author, speaker, pastor, and the founder of "Dare 2 Hear," a ministry training individuals in hearing the voice of God. Debbie is a natural encourager who is passionate about equipping individuals so they can go deeper in their relationship with God, reach their God potential, and claim their Kingdom inheritance.

Debbie's writing and teachings inspire faith and build bridges for people to believe and expect the impossible. Debbie has been equipping people to hear the voice of God in their own life and how to release the prophetic into the lives of others for over 20 years. She travels and speaks internationally. She is the author of several books including Releasing God's Heart Through Hearing His Voice, and The Gift of Prophetic Encouragement: Hearing the Words of God for Others. She is the founder and teacher of D2HTraining.com, an online course designed to equip believers in realizing God's heart. She also offers online live zoom classes and workshops.

She is married to her high school sweetheart John, they have two grown children.

To learn more, at www.debbiekitterman.com

Other Books and Material by Debbie Kitterman:

Releasing God's Heart through Hearing His Voice Training Manual. Available in English and Spanish.

Becoming Kingdom Kids Releasing God's Heart through Hearing His Voice Training Manual for kids.

The Gift of Prophetic Encouragement: Hearing the Words of God for Others

Symbolism Reference Guide and Dream Journal.

The Gift of Prophetic Encouragement Bible Study Living a Lifestyle of Encouragement

Online Training: www.d2htraining.com

Coaching, workshops, and classes available at www.debbiekitterman. com/shop.

Send all inquiries or ministry invitations to the email or address below. Or fill out the inquiry form on Debbie's website at: https://debbiekitterman. com/contact-us/

Additional copies of this book and other materials are available on our web site: www.dare2hear.com

email: info@dare2hear.com

Send a request for product inquires/orders to:

Dare 2 Hear
PO Box 50
Lyman, SC 29365

Printed in Great Britain
by Amazon

30438696R00116